THE LAST CHRISTIAN

The Release of the Siberian Seven

*Timothy Chmykhalov
with Danny Smith*

Zondervan Books
Zondervan Publishing House
Grand Rapids, Michigan

THE LAST CHRISTIAN
Copyright © 1986 by The Zondervan Corporation
Grand Rapids, Michigan

Library of Congress Cataloging in Publication Data

Chmykhalov, Timothy, 1962–
The last Christian.

1. Chmykhalov, Timothy, 1962– . 2. Refugees, Political—Soviet Union—Biography. 3. Christian—Biography—Soviet Union. 4. Persecution—Soviet Union. 5. Soviet Union—Church history—1917– . I. Smith, Danny. II Title.
DK275.C47A33   1984   272'.9'0947312   85-22716
ISBN 0-310-34021-7

All rights reserved. No part of this publication may be reproduced, stored in a retrieval system, or transmitted in any form or by any means without the prior permission of the publisher.

Edited by Daryl Townsley and Nia Jones
Designed by Judith E. Markham

Printed in the United States of America

86 87 88 89 90 91 / 10 9 8 7 6 5 4 3 2 1

Contents

Foreword   5

SIBERIA

1 Night Raid in Chernogorsk   11
2 Siberian Rainbow   18
3 The Last Christian   25
4 Under Fire   31
5 The Search for Papa Goose   37
6 "If You Believe in God, Let God Take Care of You"   40
7 My First Train Journey   45
8 Prison Scars   49
9 "There is No God!"   52
10 Secret Laws for Soviet Christians   56
11 No Other Way   64

MOSCOW

1 Incident at the Gates   71
2 Camping in the Reception Area   78
3 Depart!   83
4 Basement Refuge   87
5 The First Christmas   92
6 Laughter at Midnight   99

7	The Siberian Seven	**105**
8	US Senate Bill	**110**
9	Dead-End Street	**118**
10	Papa Threatened in Chernogorsk	**123**
11	Hunger Strike	**129**
12	Routine	**135**
13	Peace, Peace	**142**
14	The Most Unusual Visit	**148**
15	Think—Don't Think	**153**
16	The Longest Day	**160**
17	Return	**165**
18	Whirlwind Romance	**169**
19	"Don't Get Lost Again in Moscow"	**173**
20	Countdown	**179**

AMERICA

1	"It's Like a Dream"	**191**
2	No Regrets	**196**
3	Why Were We Released?	**201**

Conclusion: A Time Such as This	**204**
Acknowledgments	**207**
Notes	**211**
Appendices and a Final Note	**217**

Foreword

Timothy Chmykhalov, with the help of his friend Danny Smith, has recounted the story of the "Siberian Seven" and their long years in the American Embassy in Moscow, with great sensitivity and frankness. Timothy was only sixteen when he and his mother and the Vashchenko family found themselves "hostages of conscience." Timothy tells not only of his questionings, his frustrations, his hopes and fears, but also of his growing faith in the love and power of God. We read of his delight in prayer and Bible reading.

This is a very human account of the treatment meted out to the Seven by the puzzled American Embassy officials and the harsh treatment given to them by the atheistic Soviet regime. Some encouragement did come from such people as Dr. Andrei Sakharov and Alexandr Solzhenitsyn and Christians in the American Embassy, but leaders in Britain and America were slow to realize the desperate plight of the Seven, who waited many years for the visas necessary for emigration.

Timothy's testimony rings with confidence in God. The Soviet officials taunted him: "If you believe in God, let God take care of you." Our Lord, in His temptation by the devil and on the cross, was likewise taunted. Timothy proved that God did indeed take care of them, and he found he could say "love conquers hatred."

I am glad to commend this book and hope it will be

widely read by all who have thought of, and prayed for "prisoners of conscience" to encourage them in their praying. I also hope that it will be read and pondered by those who have never yet thanked God for what it means to live in a free country.

Jean Coggan

It is here that we see the dawn of hope: for no matter how formidably communism bristles with tanks and rockets, no matter what successes it attains in seizing the planet, it is doomed never to vanquish Christianity.

Alexandr Solzhenitsyn
The Templeton Prize Lecture
1983 London

This is the first and last time in American history that anyone will ever be allowed to stay that long in any embassy of ours anywhere in the world. You can bet on that.

US Diplomat to Timothy Chmykhalov

SIBERIA

1

Night Raid in Chernogorsk

Someone had gripped my shoulders tightly and was shaking my whole body. I could hear a human voice, but it seemed to be coming from another planet. It sounded weird, distant, and strangely like my brother Anatoly. I remained still, my eyes closed. Perhaps I could fool him. If Anatoly thought I really was asleep, maybe he would go away. Anyway, what was so important that it couldn't wait until morning?

"Wake up, Timothy, wake up."

In the dim light of our bedroom, I could vaguely distinguish the slim figure of my brother bending over me. In some distant corner of my mind, I could hear a thumping sound. It seemed too remote to try to decipher, and I turned over, brushing him aside and half mumbling that the house would have to be on fire before I was going to move.

"Tima, Tima," Again Anatoly whispered into my ear.

He never used my pet name of "Tima." Usually he called me Timothy or Tim or Timmy. Even in my dazed semiconscious state, I could sense that something was wrong. "Tima, you must wake up." His grip on my arm tightened. His words tumbled into one another. Not waiting to catch his breath, he whispered, "It's the police."

In an instant I sat upright, my eyes open. All around me the house was alive with activity. My parents, Peter and Maria Chmykhalov, were near the front door. My Aunt Anna Makarenko, Mama's sister, and my sister Nadezhda were busily trying to tidy the room. And my brothers Alexander and Anatoly were hastily trying to dress. Then the thumping sound returned. I had not been dreaming. The police were banging on the door. The shouting continued. "Open up in there. Come on, we can't wait out here all night."

We stood in a semicircle while my father unlocked the front door. Immediately three men brushed past him and strode into the center of the room. Peering past them into the dim light outside, I could make out the silhouettes of other policemen. Their boots made a sinister scraping sound on the wooden porch. I hoped they wouldn't dirty the floor too much. I knew it would be my duty tomorrow morning to clean up tonight's mess.

"Why did you come so late at night?" My father directed his questions to one of the local police sergeants whom we recognized.

The sergeant brushed my father aside and motioned him to silence. "I'll ask the questions," he answered pointedly.

The other two policemen were dressed in civilian clothes. One wore a dark brown, double-breasted raincoat that fell open at the front, revealing expensive clothes underneath. The raincoat had a modern look, and its material suggested that it was made abroad. The man remained a forceful presence at the scene but allowed the sergeant to conduct the investigation. At times he interrupted with a question or comment.

The questions were the usual ones and were repeated with boring monotony. Why couldn't we live like ordinary citizens? Why were we setting such a bad example for our children and neighbors? Did we know that we were infringing the rights of our children by forcibly teaching them about God?

I listened to Mama and Papa's response. It was a cat and mouse game. My parents' replies didn't seem to matter—the flow of questions continued unchecked. It seemed like a scene from some out-of-date black and white movie. But I knew this wasn't a drama where the players hang up their costumes and go home to normal lives. This was deadly serious.

The sergeant continued. "Why won't you accept Soviet passports?"

My father replied, "To become Soviet citizens, we would be denying God. We can't fulfill the law of God in the Soviet Union. Soviet law and God's law are in conflict with each other."

"This is an atheistic state. We don't want any believers here." The man in the fancy raincoat spoke in a tight, clipped voice with a refined accent.

"Then why can't we leave?" my father said. "We've been trying to emigrate since 1963. That's fifteen years!"

He paused for a moment. Fifteen years, I thought to myself. That's how long it's been. I was just one year old at the time. I had grown up with the hope that one day we would leave this country. Each birthday, I thought *Next year!*

"Fifteen years." My father's words rang out. "But we can't get exit visas."

I watched the man stare at my father and then turn toward our bookshelf. Casually, he ran his fingers across the titles. "That's not my problem," he said. "You must go through the proper channels."

My father raised his hands in frustration. "But every time we apply to emigrate, we are refused permission."

"We're not here to deal with exit visas. Anyway even if He agrees," the man raised his hand heavenward, "what can we do?"

I didn't see any signal, but after an exchange of words with the other policemen, the sergeant gave orders to begin searching the house. They started rummaging through our drawers, pulling them open and turning them upside down. The contents came tumbling out in untidy heaps. Very quickly, the house became a shambles. But we were getting used to this. In the past few weeks the police had raided our house several times, each time taking a few inconsequential items.

Mama kept urging the policemen to try to return things to their original place and to be careful not to break any of the fragile glass ornaments. During police raids many "accidents" occurred. Of course broken items were never replaced or money refunded.

The sergeant emphasized his right of entry into our home. "We have a court order to search these premises."

My mother said, "Does that give you the right to wake us up in the middle of the night and to turn our house upside down?"

"You people never learn." The sergeant dismissed us with a wave of his arm. Turning slowly, he moved closer to my father.

I stood near Anatoly, and we exchanged furtive glances.

"You, Peter Chmykhalov, you've been in prison twice, and you still haven't learned your lesson. I think this church-going and Bible reading has affected your mind. Only a crazy man wouldn't be grateful for the many rewards given by the party. You're an intelligent man, you could have had a good life here in Siberia if only you'd learned the error of your ways and tried to correct them. But now it's too late. Your time has run out."

He paused. His words had an edge of finality. What exactly did he mean? I knew this raid could end as abruptly as it had begun. In a matter of minutes we could be bundled into a police car and driven off into the night. But would the police arrest all of us? If so, why bother to rummage through our home? Nothing made any sense.

The sergeant glanced at the man in the raincoat. I followed his gaze but could detect no hint of their plans. The man moved toward a table in the corner of the room. Our family Bible lay open among some cutlery and other notebooks.

"A police case is being prepared against you. We're getting a prison cell ready for each of you." He turned to each of us as he named us in turn:

"Peter and Maria Chmykhalov.

"Anna Makarenko.

"Vladimir, Alexander, Timothy, and Anatoly."

Vladimir and Anatoly appeared transfixed, listening intently to the policeman.

"You can't imprison my family," my father insisted. Although his voice sounded bold, we knew the police could do anything they wished. They were above the law. He continued, "What crime have we committed? The Soviet Constitution guarantees us the right to believe."

"I'm not here to teach you how to interpret the constitution. I'm a policeman. I'm here to enforce the law. And right now you're guilty of breaking the law." The sergeant spoke with the authority and influence of his position. We could argue with him, but to little avail. "Anyway, we have secret laws on how Christians have to be controlled."

Papa's words burst out. "I know about your secret laws. Your law has little to do with justice."

The sergeant chuckled. "The law is like an animal that has been tamed. You tie a scarf over its head and put it on a leash. Wherever you pull it, it has to follow."

I caught my breath. His words frightened me. I knew exactly what he meant but I felt outraged by the injustice. I glanced around the room, and Auntie Anna gave me a reassuring nod. I yawned. Even I was surprised that my weariness had betrayed me, making me drop my guard.

The man in the raincoat jerked his head around at the sound. He walked slowly toward me.

"How old are you?"

He stared at me. Though his eyes appeared friendly, they seemed to read my innermost thoughts. My heart was thumping so loudly that I thought everyone in the room could hear it.

"I'm sixteen," I replied calmly. I refused to be intimidated. I looked back at him boldly.

"You're very tall for sixteen," he said slowly. He turned slightly toward my parents. "What will become of your young son when all of you are arrested? Have you considered the consequences of such reckless living?" The man put his hand on my shoulder.

All the blood rushed to my head, and I felt unsteady on my feet. I knew all the eyes in the room were directed toward us, but it felt as though he and I were alone on center stage.

He spoke again, as if he could read my thoughts. "Don't think anyone in the West will help you. They don't care what happens to you or your family. Believe me, it's the truth." His words were cold and chilling. "Pray to God, but it isn't going to do you any good. Here in Chernogorsk the Soviet government rules."

2

Siberian Rainbow

Siberia,[1] our homeland, is a vast, remote "continent" within the Soviet Union, encompassing eleven time zones and many language groups. The United States and half of Canada would fit easily within its boundaries. The trip of thirty-two hundred miles from Moscow to Irkutsk is like a flight from New York to Los Angeles, yet that is only half the journey across the Soviet Union. Leningrad is much closer to New York than it is to Vladivostok. Railway journeys through Siberia can be spectacularly beautiful. Cities appear almost out of nowhere and then vanish from view just as suddenly. Dwellers in such desolate places may not see visitors for months at a time.

Siberia has the largest gas and oil reserves in the world and the largest deposits of iron ore and coal. It produces half the world's gold and has diamond deposits matching those of South Africa. In 1974, Siberia replaced the United

States as the world's leading gasoline producer. Within its borders are virgin forests as large as the entire European continent. It's been claimed that if the rivers of Siberia were linked, they would circle the globe twenty-five times. Deep in the heart of Siberia abide grand riches: In addition to the gold and diamonds in Yakutia, there is also platinum, molybdenum, and wolfram. In an attempt to harness these vast resources, the Soviet government lures workers with the high wages paid in the Soviet Union. They get regular bonuses—some as high as two hundred percent. Still much of this cold "continent" with its unusually harsh climate remains uninhabited, and Siberia's population is only about thirty-three million people.

In the eighteenth century, scientist Mikhail Lomonosov prophesied that Siberia's natural resources and riches would provide the Soviet Union with its source of might and power. Author Maxim Gorky, on the other hand, called Siberia "a land of death and chains." Probably the truth lies somewhere between these extremes.

Part of the government's solution to the problem of harnessing Siberia's resources has been to organize a workforce of labor-camp prisoners. The Soviet government has always used this form of free labor, and it is conservatively estimated that one or two million inmates of Soviet labor camps have been legally condemned to work in Siberia. Reports of slave labor being used to work on the Siberian gas pipeline to Europe have been headlines in the Western press and have claimed that Christians and political prisoners have been put to work on the construction site. Certainly, no one in the Soviet Union ever reads any such reports in the Soviet press, yet most people know about the labor camps.

Some prisoners serve out terms of exile near my

hometown of Chernogorsk. Journalist Yuri Belov served part of his fifteen-year sentence nearby, living in forced exile.[2] Exile can be as difficult as a term in a prison or labor camp because there is no regular source of income, no certainty of finding work, no ready supply of food, and no apparent friends since some of the local people are naturally cautious of prisoners.

Chernogorsk is known as the "Black Mountain" and is situated in the southwestern region of Siberia, some two thousand miles east of Moscow, quite near the Mongolian border, immediately north of Tibet. Abakan, a larger and older city eighteen kilometers southwest of Chernogorsk, is generally easier to find. The rolling hills of the Sayan mountain range toward the south provide pleasant surroundings. From the top floors of the newer high-rise apartment blocks, the snowy white peaks are visible.

Chernogorsk was registered as a town in 1938. It is typical of many other small towns in Siberia. Most of the older houses—such as ours, with four rooms on one floor—are built of wood. As the city expanded, concrete high-rise apartment blocks, some five or six stories tall were erected. Today, Chernogorsk has about 300,000 residents almost all of whom are employed in the factories in town.

A small coal field near Chernogorsk, which was developed after World War II, provided the town with its main industry. At that time, most of the coal miners were prisoners from the labor camps. One large camp housed Germans expelled from the Ukraine and the Volga region after the Nazis had retreated; another camp, political prisoners who were serving sentences as long as twenty-five years; a third camp, women who were common criminals.

My mother, Maria Petrovna Makarenko, was born in 1922, the second child of a large family. She grew up near Ochury, south of the Black Mountain, and for a time in the early forties, worked in a grain warehouse. As a young woman with a bleak future, she became depressed and contemplated suicide, but a Christian couple, also working at the warehouse, loaned her their New Testament. Reading the Scriptures gave her hope and the hint of a new life.

In 1943, her younger sister, Anna, age fifteen, traveled to the new settlement formed at Black Mountain and began work at the coal mine. Around this time their father died, and in February 1946, my mother joined her sister. She found a job working underground in Mine Nine as a *motoriskava* operating the conveyor belt, which transports the coal to its base.

Although Mama's parents were not believers themselves, they had strong Christian principles, and even before Mama's conversion, the miners had nicknamed her "the Baptist."

Both sisters found their new life very difficult in the Black Mountain settlement, and sometimes Mama prayed that God would take her home.

The coal mine at Black Mountain valley might seem like an unusual setting for a romance, but Maria met and fell in love with a short, wiry coal miner, four years her junior, named Peter Sergevich Chmykhalov. Papa was a war veteran seeking a new life. In 1950, they were married when Mama was twenty-eight. They built a house at Twentieth Khakassia Year Street in the settlement at Mine Nine where Mama worked. This settlement developed into a suburb of Chernogorsk and was called Chernogorsk—1.

Peter and Maria named their first child Nadezhda; she

was to be the only girl in a family of five. Two years later, in 1954, Vladimir was born. Mama's sisters Anna and Katia, and their mother, Yelena Makarenko, also lived at the house on Khakassia Street.

Katia was a young lady of twenty-three when she first began to attend the services held by believers in the town. She persuaded Mama and Papa to attend one of the services, and it was the turning point in their lives. Mama said, "We were so moved by the experience that we decided to follow God." The meeting, held in one of the believers' homes, had been lead by one of the elders and lasted several hours. Many hymns and gospel songs were sung, and several sermons were given by the leaders. One sermon text was from the sixth chapter of Romans: "The wages of sin is death, but the gift of God is eternal life in Christ Jesus our Lord" (NIV).

Mama has since described her experience: "The service made a big impact on us. The explanations by the brethren who preached and the singing of the hymns deeply touched our sinful souls. We believed that the Savior had redeemed us at a costly price and that He had forgiven all our sins. We surrendered fully to Christ and soon afterward accepted water baptism. From that time we have tried to keep His commandments, although we often transgress, sin, and fall, with God's help we stand up and go ever forward."

By the end of the year, all of Mama's family had become believers, including her elderly mother. My brother Anatoly was born two years after this, and in 1960, they had Alexander, their third son. Finally two years later, Mama gave birth to their last child.

I was born in Chernogorsk's only maternity hospital. I was actually born during the early hours of May 1, but many people in the USSR are superstitious and consider

May a very unlucky month. The nurse in charge of registering births told my parents, "We want to wish him luck so we will record his birth on April 30." So I was born lucky, and my birthday became April 30. I was named Timothy Petrovich Chmykhalov.

Petrovich is not merely my middle name but is known as a patronymic and is derived from my father's first name, Peter. "Ovich" means "son of," so I am known as Timothy, the son of Petro. My mother's name is Maria Petrovna Chmykhalova because "ovna" means "daughter of" and our grandfather's name was also Peter. Last names also have a feminine form. All the girls in our family take the name Chmykhalova while the men are Chmykhalov.

Patronymics are very important since there are no real equivalents to Mr., Mrs., and Miss in Russian. It is common practice to address persons who are not relatives, close friends, or children by their first name and their patronymic. In the Soviet Union I would always be addressed Timothy Petrovich. This custom is continued when someone is known well, so we do not have difficulty deciding when to drop the formal surname and be on a first name basis.

Although Katia married and moved away to her own home, my grandmother and Aunt Anna continued to live with us, and all of us children grew to love them both dearly. It was from Anna, our beloved Nana, that we learned the stories of the Bible, which she filled with wonder and excitement. It was a common sight for our Nana to be surrounded by all of us children, staring wide-eyed as we learned about the daring exploits of Daniel or the courage of David. Nana was generally busy with some housework and chores, but she always had time for us little ones.

Despite hardship and poverty, we were a close-knit family, drawing strength, support, and encouragement from each other. We all attended the local church services held in people's homes. We didn't see ourselves as leaders or visionaries, we were simply Christians, who wished to serve God, to follow peacefully His teachings, and to live together as a Christian family, worshiping our Lord.

3

The Last Christian

I was born in 1962, a time of great persecution for all believers inside the Soviet Union. The crackdown began in the late fifties when President Nikita Khrushchev declared war on believers. He personally swore to wipe out Christianity. "The last Christian," he thundered, "will become a relic to be ridiculed on public television." Perhaps he thought it would be easy after glimpsing some Christians, languishing idly at the edge of any firm commitment, questioning whether God was dead or merely silent.

Khrushchev declared, "Our country has become a country of atheism. The vast majority of the Soviet people are convinced atheists. They live not for the sake of Paradise in Heaven, but for the sake of Communism on Earth."[3] And at the Twenty-second Congress of the Communist Party of the Soviet Union, the party worked out a program for building a fully Communist, atheistic society. Khrushchev said that in the new society there would not be a single believer; the plan was to eradicate all believers in Christ. The text from the "Documents of the Twenty-second Congress of the Communist Party of the Soviet Union" show how they intended to achieve this. It states, "To eliminate religious belief, believers should not be allowed to spread their religion and points of view, especially among young people and children."

The Kremlin's first order was that all churches should obey the authorities and register, and registration regulations (1929 law, articles 2,5,6) were devised that gave the Soviet State power to control all legally existing places of worship. To implement these controls, two official organizations were created: the Council for the Affairs of the Russian Orthodox Church, and the Council for the Affairs of the Religious Cults, responsible for all other denominations. In a secret decree N394 (not for publication), the chief executive for the "Affairs of Religious Cults" received the power to appoint church elders and pastors in registered churches to ensure impartiality. The chief executive was to be a Communist and an atheist. This plan became "A Law concerning some Religious Cults" and was accepted by all registered churches. When a church registered, its leadership was placed under the control of the state.

This was, of course, a list of conditions for registration. These conditions appalled most believers in Chernogorsk but caused a conflict that has continued to this day:

First, we could not worship God as we chose.

Second, we were not allowed to teach children about God, even in our own homes. Sunday schools were forbidden.

Third, our preaching and evangelism were limited and sometimes illegal. Printing, producing, and distributing Christian literature (including Bibles, hymn books, prayer books) was not allowed.

Fourth, we were forbidden to teach and preach vigilance over members, knowing where they were at all times, and visitors to the church were to be reported to the authorities.[4]

Christians in Chernogorsk were faced with this question: Should we register our church and follow these mandates, or should we become law breakers by refusing to register? We were in the position of Peter and John when the Sanhedrin ordered them not to preach in the name of Jesus. Faced with that command, Peter and John replied, "We must obey God, rather than men."[5] Although Christians who refused to register turned their church members into outlaws whom the Soviet authorities were quick to pursue, we, nevertheless, refused to register. Jesus Christ was our Lord and supreme authority, not the state.

According to John Barron in *The KGB:* "The first chairman of the Council of Affairs of the Russian Orthodox Church was a KVD general, G. C. Karpov. (KVD was the forerunner of the KGB). Ever since, the regulatory councils have been dominated by the KGB."[6] In fact Karpov worked fairly happily with the Orthodox church. But in 1960, he was replaced by V. Kuroyedov, a much harder man. In 1966 the two groups controlling church affairs for the Orthodox church and the other denominations merged into the Council for Religious Affairs, and Kuroyedov became the head of this new merged council.

Some indication of the extent of the pressure against Christians is revealed by a questionnaire given to school children in Prienai in 1973. According to *The Chronicle of the Lithuanian Catholic Church,* "after filling out this questionnaire dictated by the teacher in the classroom, the students must sign it and give it to the teacher."[7]

1. What do you value a person for? For diligence, frankness, fairness, courtesy, collectivism, appearance, scholarship, talent, religious devotion?
2. How do you rate adults who go to church? (Positively, negatively, no opinion)
3. How do you rate students who go to church? (Positively, negatively, no opinion)
4. Do you agree with the opinion of believers that prayer and belief improve a person? (I agree, I do not agree, I don't know)
5. Some parents send their children to church. What is your attitude toward the behavior of such parents? (Positive, negative, no opinion)
6. In school it is affirmed that prayer and a belief in God contradict science. What is your opinion? (I agree, I disagree, I partly agree)
7. Are church holidays observed in your family? (Yes, no, sometimes)
8. Are there Icons in your apartment or house? (Yes, no)
9. Is it the custom in your family to cross yourself before and after meals? (Yes, no)
10. Do they pray in your family? (Yes, no, sometimes)
11. In your home are there sacramental wafers on Christmas Eve? (Yes, no)
12. Does a priest visit your home? (Yes, no)
13. Do you believe in God, angels, the devil? (Yes, no, sometimes)
14. When was the last time you went to church? (5,4,3,2,1 years ago, recently)

15. Did you take First Communion? (Yes, no)
16. Who prepared you for First Communion/for Confirmation? (Relatives, aunts, ministers, a priest)
17. Do you like atheistic books and talks on atheistic subjects? (Yes, no, such topics have not yet come up)
18. The church preaches love for one's parents and abstaining from evil. Therefore it does no damage. (I agree, I disagree, I don't know)
19. The laws of nature are immutable. Therefore miracles cannot happen. (I agree, I disagree, I don't know)
20. Are your parents believers? (They are believers, they are nonbelievers, they have doubts)
21. Why do you go to church? (Out of conviction, because prompted by parents, because it is interesting)

Because of the pressure against Christians, many Christian leaders and Christian families all over the Soviet Union believed that God was calling them to leave the Soviet Union. This was their understanding of scriptural teachings and biblical prophecies (Revelation 18:4). But as they pursued emigration through normal, and legal, channels, the authorities pursued them, using the Criminal Code to convict many innocent victims. Though the Soviet Constitution does not have a specific policy on emigration, the implication of many Soviet statements is that anyone who chooses can leave the country. Of course, this is a fantasy. On the contrary, Christians (and others) are imprisoned if they make known their desire to emigrate, though they are convicted on various drummed-up charges.

Our family was caught in this crossfire. We wanted to live together as a Christian family and we wanted to emigrate. We did not seek emigration because we wanted luxuries, pleasures, or a life of ease in the West, but because we wished to live for Christ. In the Soviet Union, this freedom was not allowed.

4

Under Fire

The early sixties was the dark age of Krushchev's antireligious campaign. One Sunday morning in 1962, the year I was born, my father was leading a house fellowship service. Alexander, my two-year-old brother, was sitting beside him as he read from the Scriptures. Suddenly the service was disrupted. Without any warning, the local KGB chief Ivan Ikonikov and a gang of thugs burst in, overturning tables and wreaking havoc as they stormed toward the front of the room where my father sat.

Ikonikov was tall, dark-haired, and unafraid of anyone. He clearly enjoyed his work. He seized my father by the throat and began to choke him as Alexander clung to my father's hand, crying and screaming in fright. Ikonikov then began to drag my father toward the exit. He pushed him against the wall and again began to squeeze his throat. In a frenzy, Alexander swung his little arms, punching the KGB chief with all his might. "Papa, Papa," he screamed.

All around the room the local thugs were swearing, tearing up Bibles, and jostling people while my mother cradled me, her nine-month-old babe, and chased after the KGB chief, who had taken Papa and Alexander outside. As my mother reached the entrance, Ikonikov tried to close the door, but somehow she managed to get outside. Turning quickly, Ikonikov seized Alexander, who immediately started screaming even louder.

Mama cried out, "Ivan Romanovich, why are you choking and frightening a child? Is this allowed?"

Ikonikov began grappling with her outside the building as my father staggered back, gasping for breath. Mama recalls, "Then he swung and his arm hit my baby."

The force of the blow sent me reeling, but my mother clutched me tightly as she fell. I was stunned but unharmed, while my mother suffered severe bruising. I was only a babe, but I had a full voice and raised the alarm as loudly as my lungs would allow as Mama tried to restrain her attacker. When she tried to pick herself up, he struck her on the arms. Finally he left her to supervise the arrest of the Christians who were being handed summons, which had been hastily written up by the KGB man and his "assistant."

My mother tried to compose herself, and still clutching me to her body, called out to him, "What kind of law gives you the right to beat up a child like this?" Then she returned indoors with me, and with the windows wide open, she began to read from the Gospels as the police van was loaded up with believers. They were taken to the police station where they were held for a few days and fined.

Early one morning an ambulance drew up outside our home. A man with a white coat stepped from the vehicle accompanied by Ivan Ikonikov. They opened the gate and walked up the path toward the front door. My mother, who had risen early that morning to milk our cow, blocked Ikonikov's path and said, "Where do you think you're going? Everyone's asleep."

Ikonikov pushed her aside and entered our house. My grandmother and aunt were sleeping in the hallway. He walked over to Auntie's bed, grabbed hold of the blanket, and jerked it off. Thinking one of the children was joking with her, Auntie clutched the blanket. Ikonikov called out loudly, "Get up, get up."

My grandmother and Auntie awoke, and so did all the children. There was a lot of noise and commotion. The KGB chief started to swear and curse; some of my brothers began to cry. When asked why he had come, Ikonikov replied that he was there to arrest Anna Makarenko. He said, "She's crazy. She claims to believe in God. The streets aren't safe with such people walking around. We're going to put her in a psychiatric hospital. That's where she belongs."

But my aunt and grandmother argued with him and his assistant. Eventually he withdrew, and the psychiatric hospital was cheated of a prisoner.

Throughout 1962, these incidents continued relentlessly; Mama recalls many traumatic times. The leaders of the services were fined, and the meetings were disrupted. Once one woman had her dress torn in a scuffle. Her panties were ripped off, and she was bundled into a police car and driven off. On another occasion Ikonikov's thugs began grappling with some of the believers while Ikonikov grabbed my Aunt Anna by the sleeve.

Mama said, "Her dress was ripped at the shoulder. My little daughter Nadezhda, aged ten years old, clung to

Anna's hand and screamed. So Ikonikov swung his hand and hit my little daughter. That is just what happened."

That same year Ikonikov burst into an Easter service, ripped up Bibles and hymn books, and overturned tables while the congregation was chased outside and forced to sweep the street.

Thugs and hooligans were encouraged to smash windows of Christians' homes and buildings where services were held. One sunny Sunday morning, about seventy Christians were crowded into a small house for their morning worship service. Suddenly, the local mine rescue and fire brigade chief, Sokolov, burst in.

"Disperse," he shouted.

No one moved.

"I declare war on you!" he bellowed and left the room.

Outside the building, Sokolov ordered the mine rescue truck to ram the wall. The impact shook the little house to its foundations. Plaster flew off the walls, glass was forced out of the window panes, and a mirror fell to the floor. The congregation, however, resumed singing and praying. Then they heard the sound of the fire engine siren. Firemen trampled across the garden, and standing by a window, they turned their hoses on the Christians inside. Children shrieked as the powerful jets hit them and flooded the room, soaking and ruining books and Bibles. But somehow the believers managed to remain firm. Eventually the fire engine was completely drained of water.

The Soviet machine was now in gear and sweeping everything in its path. War had been declared, quite literally. Christians all over the Soviet Union faced the same fate. They were fired from their jobs, fined, arrested, imprisoned; church services were raided by police and tear-gassed; even children were taken from their parents; Christians were forced to attend reeducation lectures.

As a result of such persecution, many believers felt that God was leading them to take two steps. First they felt that they should communicate with Christians in the West to inform their fellow brethren of the problems they were facing and to ask for help. Secondly, some came to feel that God was calling them to leave the Soviet Union.

By the end of 1962, the situation in Chernogorsk was very severe. Many Christian homes had been invaded; twenty-one people had been arrested and placed in prison, camp, or exile for practicing their Christian faith. Many children from Christian homes had been taken away and placed in state orphanages to be indoctrinated with atheistic propaganda. This time the Christians in Chernogorsk made a dramatic and historic decision: they organized the first public demonstration inside the Soviet Union.

On January 3, 1963, thirty-two Christians from Chernogorsk burst into the American Embassy in Moscow to appeal for help from those in the embassy and to send telegrams to Christians in the Free World. What a commotion there was! Telexes and wire services from the international media buzzed. The Christians from Siberia were now on center stage and had turned the spotlight on themselves.

This demonstration created a sensation in the West; with front page articles in the national press, it was the first indication to those in the West that the Christian faith had survived the atheistic assault.

Kuznetsov, the Soviet minister from the Ministry of Foreign Affairs, pleaded ignorance to the Siberians' claims of persecution. An investigation followed and promises were made. None of the thirty-two were imprisoned immediately upon their return home, but few of Minister Kuznetsov's promises were fulfilled. Instead, the crackdown continued relentlessly. After three months it was apparent that nothing had changed and nothing would, except for the worst. The assurances we had received from Moscow in 1963 were to be the first of many promises and guarantees from the Soviet government. And like all of the others, they proved to be false. Soviet promises are fabricated specifically to fool the innocent bystander. To those who know and have experienced real life inside the USSR, these fabrications are merely painted facades.

Two decades later during another crisis at the American Embassy, I had to make the crucial decision of whether to risk believing hollow Soviet promises.

5

The Search for Papa Goose

Each of us shared responsibility around the home and was assigned jobs to do.

I was three years old when I was taken to the fields to work. Our field was divided up into rows that were apportioned among us according to age. The older ones received more rows; the younger ones less. Since I was younger than everyone else, I was given the least number. Mama and all the children would start weeding the potatoes, but I would cry and create some disturbance. I didn't like to work and would much rather play, so I would wait until everyone was working and when I thought it was clear, I would try to run away from the work. Then Mama would give me a little spank and send me home.

Being the youngest, I was spoiled by my grandmother. I was her favorite, and she would always find some excuse for me to stay behind with her. I loved to sit at her feet and listen to her stories about the famine and the war. I was fascinated by what I heard.

One of my chores was to watch over the geese while they grazed. Usually Alexander and I shared this duty.

Once when I was four, Alex and I were caught in a terrible thunderstorm. As we hurried home, it began to rain very hard, and a strong wind kept blowing the geese over. The rain completely soaked us. When we got home, we realized that the goose we called "Papa" was missing. We children immediately organized a search party.

Beyond our settlement, some holes a meter deep had been dug in the ground for telephone posts. We searched in those holes and eventually heard the sound of Papa Goose coming from one of them. His wings were stuck in the mud, and he couldn't fly out. We tried to think of ways to release him, but there was nothing we could use to pull him out of the deep hole.

Then somebody had a brainstorm.

Vladimir, my eldest brother, was the tallest and thinest of us all. We decided to lower him into the hole headfirst so that he could grab the goose with his hands. Then we would pull them both out together. We held onto his legs, and slowly Vladimir's head and chest disappeared into the hole. He managed to grab the goose. But the heavy rain had made the ground very soft and slippery. We slipped in the mud, and as we came tumbling down in the slush, Vladimir plunged into the hole.

We were all very frightened, and I started to scream. So did the others. The hole was filling up with rain water and Vladimir was beginning to splutter and choke.

We decided to make one last attempt. We pulled with all our might, and in a few seconds, Vladimir and Papa Goose were above ground. We ran back to the house and reunited our family of geese, who immediately began to cackle together. All of us were soaked to the skin, but extremely relieved to be home safe.

Since much of our food came from what we planted, we welcomed the rains. But heavy downpours could cause problems.

To live and to give to others, we reared cattle, sometimes as many as nine head, including calves. In the USSR, it's very hard to get fresh milk, so a cow is a valuable possession. My older brothers had the responsibility of tending the cattle, and as I grew older, I also joined them, pleased to be in the company of the older boys.

Sometimes when we were out with the cows, we would lead them toward Mine Nine. Close-by there was a reservoir where we used to bathe. The fine coal remained in the tank, and when we got home we would still be dirty from the coal and would need two or three baths to get clean again. We were young at the time, and it seemed only natural for us and our friends (children from believer's families who lived nearby) to swim in the nude. But as we grew older, we were embarrassed and stopped swimming in the tank. Then we used to go swimming with our friends in the Yenisei River, fifteen miles to the east of our hometown.

6

"If You Believe in God, Let God Take Care of You"

My early childhood memories are filled with scenes of police harassing Christians during church services, even on Christmas Day. Local police and government officials seemed to take delight in ridiculing and mocking us. "There go the slaves of God," they would chant as we walked past. I recall these incidents occurring throughout my childhood. The taunts continued in school when the teachers encouraged fellow pupils to goad me because of my faith.

Our family was well acquainted with the midnight world of the Soviet prison network that Alexandr Solzhenitsyn has described as "the Gulag archipelago." It was as though we had been charged in some invisible court and given a sentence that was to be served all through life.

I was six years old when a friend of Auntie's called at our home. The lady was out of breath and was clearly frightened. She clutched Auntie Anna's bag in her hand. "Your Nyanka has been arrested," the lady said and handed over the bag.

Alexander, aged eight, took the bag and pressed it against his chest. He fell on a box and started to sob, "Auntie, Auntie, where are you now?" All of us children loved Auntie, but Alexander was her favorite nephew, and he loved her specially.

Anna Makarenko was put on trial with several other believers. Just before the judges entered the courtroom, the police chased us children out of the room. But we sneaked back inside and crawled under the benches. If they had seen us, we would have been dragged from the courtroom. The charges against my aunt and the others were more or less the same: they were dangerous criminals; they preached heresy; they lived without a Soviet passport; worse, they wanted to go abroad to our enemies.

As the trial proceeded, many of the people in the courtroom shouted, "Put her in prison." Some yelled, "Shoot her." Others said, "Send them to the polar bears . . . let them live with the bears."

Anna was convicted and received a one-year sentence. After the judge delivered the sentence, three policemen led our Anna by foot to the KPZ temporary detaining cell about five hundred meters from the courtroom. One policeman blocked our way so that we were unable to follow, but another said, "Let the kids go, if they want to." And so it was that all we little ones went together with Auntie and managed to say good-by. All the believers who attended the trial followed behind, and some cried, both relatives and friends. When Auntie was led through the gates of KPZ, we all stood behind the gates and cried as we watched her disappear inside the building. The policeman chased us away and closed the gate. And so we returned home, walking through the streets with tear-stained eyes.

Our Anna was held in Minusinsk prison for several months. During this time, we cut back on our food so that we could send her food parcels, because we knew prison food was very bad. We also saved some chocolates and other delicacies for her. The parcels were given to one of the administrators of the jail, a man named Misha. He was also responsible for granting visits, but we were not given a single visit during this period. Eventually when we did get to see her, we learned that she had not received any of the food parcels or the money that we sent for her.

The rest of her one-year sentence was served at a camp for women prisoners at Reshoty. On her last day at this camp, Blinov, the commandant, decided to play a cruel joke on her. He led her outside the camp zone and asked her, "Will you now take a Soviet passport and agree to be a Soviet citizen?"

Our Anna replied, "I cannot be a Soviet citizen. I am unable to keep atheist law. I am a believer."

Blinov then called one of the guards and said to him, "She still hasn't learned her lesson. Take her back to the camp. She must serve a longer sentence." Wearily, Anna picked up her few meager belongings and trudged back into the camp complex. But as she walked past the gate of the camp, Blinov screamed, "Okay, let her go home."

Usually the camp provides an escort or transport to the nearest train station at Tunguska. From Tunguska, she would board another train to the Reshoty town center where the labor camp's administrative office is situated. At the office, Anna would be given a ticket back to Chernogorsk, her earnings from camp, and money that we had sent to her—about thirty-eight rubles. This was the Soviet law. But Blinov refused to provide transport or an escort. Instead, he sneered, "Let God take care of you." So Anna was left to make the journey to Tunguska and on to Reshoty by herself.

A heavy snowstorm made the journey on foot very difficult. Up ahead, Anna saw two rough-looking men from the men's camp. All around was dense forest, with snow piling up on the railway track where Anna was stumbling on her way. Feeling very alone and nervous, she passed the two men, praying each step of the way for protection. Bundled up in old clothes from the camp, she must have seemed like a thin, exhausted ex-prisoner—the men allowed her to pass unharmed.

The train from Tunguska to the Reshoty camp center did not leave until six o'clock the following morning. But again her prayers were answered, and she was given shelter for the night by a kindly lady near the station. But when she reached the camp's administrative office in Reshoty, they refused to help her. One official again mocked her, "If you believe in God, let God take care of you."

So Auntie left the office and walked about the streets praying to God for guidance and help. And again God answered her prayers. She returned to the lady at the train station in Tunguska, and once again this woman took pity and helped Anna sell some belongings to raise money for the journey home. On the train a woman and child befriended her and shared their food with her for the three days it took to reach Chernogorsk.

When Auntie returned home and shared her stories with us, we became very angry with those people who had treated our Anna so badly. But she said to us, "No, you must not be angry with them. You must pity them and pray for them. The hatred that they feel has distorted their true selves. They take their vengeance out on innocent people like us and delight in it. They do not know God, and this causes their hatred to increase and overflow. We must pray that God will change their hearts. If we pray for them and love them, then the chain of hatred is broken. If we also hate and pass on their hatred, then we fall victim to the evil that has overtaken the world. This is our strength as believers. This is the lesson we have to teach the Communists. Love conquers hatred."

That first night we praised God together in a feast of celebration. We had Auntie back home, and she was safe. God had answered our prayers and provided protection.

During the next few days, Anna told us more about her experiences in camp and on the way home. "I was in a desperate situation," she said. "I felt utterly helpless and completely alone. Blinov, the camp commandant thought he was challenging God, but he was merely entrusting me to His care. I didn't know how help would come but I continued to trust in Him. I was abandoned into the care of God."

My aunt's experiences and her attitude toward her captors had a profound effect on me. I ached for her. But I felt privileged to know how real God had been to her. I thought about this for several days afterward, and I prayed for faith like hers. Such memories live with you a long time.

7

My First Train Journey

Back in Chernogorsk, Anna Makarenko found she was unemployable. There were many jobs available, but not for her.

She was rearrested a few months later for the same offense: refusing to be a Soviet citizen. Once again, she was convicted and sentenced to one year in prison. According to Soviet law, prisoners are not permitted to return to the same camp for internment for a second term, but my aunt was sent back to the camp in Reshoty where she had already served.

Then late one night in May 1969 when I was seven years old, there came the knock on the door we all had been dreading. Framed in the doorway were several policemen. Beyond them in the street, we saw a police car. The driver kept the motor running. Both Mama and Papa were placed under arrest, even though they had young children at home. The official charge was for passport violations, but in reality they were arrested because they were outspoken Christians and active in the local church. I was too young to understand this and assumed that my parents must be criminals for the police to be so angry with them. I dared not ask what crime they had committed.

The police permitted us one final prayer together. I felt as if all my feelings and emotions had been drained from my body. I wondered if I would ever see Papa again. Horrifying images appeared in my mind. In despair and foreboding, I sank to my knees beside the rest of my family. Our prayers mingled with tears as we placed our parents in the safe hands of God. We were filled with anguish; our minds raced with unspeakable thoughts.

Before he went my father hugged me, and something of the peace of God exchanged between father and son. The presence of God was to be our inheritance.

My father was sent to Minusinsk prison for investigation and then received a one-year sentence. He was told by the judge that he was being tried because he had requested permission to emigrate. The judge added, "You are on trial for breaking the passport regulations, because you have no passport, according to article 198 of the Soviet Criminal Code." At that point, my father took his passport out of his pocket and placed it on the judge's table. But the judge refused to accept this in the trial proceedings and sentenced Papa to one-year's exile.

My mother was taken to KPZ cell at Chernogorsk. Her health deteriorated while in custody, and she was threatened with internment in a psychiatric hospital but received a one-year sentence for passport violations. This sentence was suspended because of her weak physical condition, and she returned home.

When our parents were away, our grandmother looked after us, though she was seventy years old and unwell. After Mama came back, we still found life difficult, but somehow we managed to survive, helped at times by the Christians in Chernogorsk.

Papa and two other believers from Chernogorsk were sent first to Krasnoyarsk and then assigned to a work project near Barnaul in the Altai territory, about 540 kilometers west of Chernogorsk. Living conditions were grim, and the work was hard. Families of prisoners are permitted an extended visit. I was seven when Mama took Alexander, Anatoly, and me for a two-week visit to see Papa in Barnaul. We traveled with local believers who were visiting their grandparents in the city. I was very excited. I was looking forward very much to seeing Papa again, and it was also the first time I had ever traveled in a train.

We left late at night in an almost empty carriage, so we children soon enjoyed ourselves crawling along the berths. The carriage had just returned from the repair shop and was in a filthy state. Until midnight we crawled along the berths and ran through the car going to sleep wherever we were. At daylight Mama woke us and began to wash us, beginning with the oldest and ending with the youngest.

We waited a day to change trains at Novokuznetsk and reached Barnaul before dawn the next morning. Then we rode in a crowded bus to the visitor's dormitory, where the person on duty tried at first to refuse to let us children stay.

When Papa returned from his day's work, we all rushed to him and hugged him. He looked paler and thinner than I remembered him and tired. But I was so pleased to see him that I quickly forgot these things. We strolled through the woods to the river Barnaulka, about three kilometers from the settlement. All around was forest, and we saw a squirrel and watched it jump from tree to tree. We swam in the river, with me on Papa's back where it was deeper because I was unable to swim. In the following days we often walked to the Barnaulka to swim, explore the woods, and chase squirrels.

We also visited the plant where Papa worked because it was interesting for us to ride around the city in the tram. Papa worked at all sorts of jobs. One time when we were in the tram, rogues or hooligans began to follow us to beat us and take our last copecks. We dashed from one tram to another, riding around for four or five hours to get away from them. Then we returned to our room.

After two weeks, the time came for us to leave. Papa accompanied us to the train. Everyone said good-by and Anatoly hugged Papa and began to cry. We got in the carriage, and everyone began to look out of the windows to wave and to cry. When the train pulled away, Papa ran along the platform and waved. We screamed for him to stay where he was, but he ran all the way down the platform. When the platform ended he ran a bit further, but then the train began to move faster, and Papa was left behind. Everyone cried because we could no longer see Papa, and he was no longer with us. Probably Papa cried too. This episode was so painful that I want to cry now as I recall it.

8

Prison Scars

After my father's release, he returned to work at the coal mine and continued his involvement with the local church, although he knew how dangerous this could be.

One day in 1972 when I was ten, my father had a premonition that he would be arrested. As he stepped off the bus on his way to work in the morning, he noticed a police car following him. Within minutes he was picked up. He was rearrested, charged, and sentenced to another year in a hard labor camp.

Prison is an experience that reaches into many Soviet lives.[8] In Solzhenitsyn's words, "It is the secret bond of grief that unites them."

It is a trauma from which some people never fully recover; they are scarred emotionally for the rest of their lives. But through the power of God, healing is possible.

Throughout my childhood, I had dark visions of what the

inside of a prison cell would be like. I knew many Christians who had endured severe punishments for their faith. Some had entered prison as healthy young men to emerge several years later only a shadow of their former selves. These thoughts troubled me. Sometimes I had nightmares, but fortunately, I could never remember my dreams when I awoke. All I knew was that I had had a bad dream.

In *The Gulag Archipelago,*[9] Alexandr Solzhenitsyn writes about conditions in Minusinsk Prison some years before my father was sent there.[10] He also describes an incident in the forties when the prisoners in Minusinsk had been cooped up for an entire year.[11]

While Solzhenitsyn's pen has provided a panoramic view of the Soviet prison network, other writers have also made valuable contributions, many from their own personal experience.

In June 1970, Eduard Kuznetsov, together with a group of Young Soviet Jews, was arrested for attempting to hijack a plane to fly to Sweden. The group was put on trial and sentenced to death. After a world outcry, the death sentence was commuted to fifteen years' imprisonment. Kuznetsov managed to smuggle out of confinement his *Prison Diaries*. Here he described some of the horrors he had seen while adrift in the prison camps.

Some prisoners carried out unbelievable acts of self-mutilation, not because they were "tragic victims of the regime, its hunted and its persecuted, but because they had been reduced to the level of masochism."

> The destructive element within them boils over in a rage of impotence and is transformed into fits of hatred and feverish dreams of revenge on the prison governor; as soon

as they realize that they can't get their teeth into his throat, they finally turn on themselves.

I have many times witnessed some of the most fantastic incidences of self-mutilation. I have seen convicts swallow huge numbers of nails and quantities of barbed wire; I have seen them swallow mercury thermometers, pewter tureens (after first breaking them up into "edible" proportions), chess pieces, dominoes, needles, ground glass, spoons, knives and many other similar objects; I have seen convicts sew up their mouths and eyes with thread or wire; sew rows of buttons to their bodies; or nail their testicles to a bed, swallow a nail bent like a hook, and then attach the hook to the door by way of a thread so that the door cannot be opened without pulling the "fish" inside out. I have seen convicts cut open the skin on their arms and legs and peel it off as if it were a stocking; or cut out lumps of flesh (from their stomach or their legs), roast them and eat them; or let the blood drip from a slit vein into a tureen, crumble bread crumbs into it, and then gulp it down like a bowl of soup; or cover themselves with paper and set fire to themselves; or cut off their fingers, or their nose, or ears, or penis . . .[12]

Anatoly Marchenko, another prisoner who has spent more time in prison than at liberty, also witnessed similar incidents. His book *My Testimony* is one of the first accounts (and still among the most powerful) of conditions in the post-Stalin prison system.

He writes, "What had I been reduced to by a few months in prison. . . . A man pours out his blood before my eyes and I lick my soup bowl clean and think only about how long it is till the next meal. Did anything human remain in me, or in any of us, in that prison?"[13]

9

"There is No God!"

Increasingly, school became a problem for me. I enjoyed the classes and studied math, science, and literature. I felt the discipline of studying was good for me. I found geography very interesting and imagined myself traveling to different cities and exploring their history. But I was known as a believer, and because of this, I was frequently bullied and ridiculed in class. The teachers tried to argue with me about God, hoping to make me renounce my faith. One teacher said to me, "Where is God? Have you ever seen God? Men have been in sputniks into space and have walked on the moon. No one has seen God. There is no God. It's a fairy tale."

The teachers also encouraged other pupils to taunt me and to beat me. And when I was being bullied by some of the students, the teachers never stopped them or tried to help me. As a result, I couldn't finish school.

Despite these problems, my childhood was a happy one. There was always a lot of work to do at home, but I was lazy and sometimes tried to sneak off to play with my friends or to go for long walks by myself.

We were always in need of hay to feed our cattle. Once when I was eight, we had been offered as much hay as we wanted. There were just two problems. First, we had to mow the field by ourselves. Second, the field was five kilometers away. As we only had one bicycle, we walked to the field. When we had finished mowing the hay, we still had to rake it and place it together in sheaves.

On the last morning I thought I would escape from this work, but Mama forced me to go to the field with the family. I began to rake the hay very quickly—and very badly—wishing that this chore would be over soon. Mama noticed this and scolded me. She then asked me to rake the area again. I didn't want to do it, and we argued. I turned my back to begin walking away from the field when suddenly Mama spanked me with the rake; the handle of the rake broke in two!

I grew tall and straight. I had many friends and enjoyed playing with them; most of my friends were Christian young people from the local church. I had many hobbies and enjoyed collecting things, such as stamps and coins. I was proudest of one coin that had survived the prerevolutionary days of the czar.

As a teenager, I became interested in journalism and photography. For a while I considered a career in journalism. I enjoyed taking photographs and soon began to develop my prints in a makeshift studio at the back of our home. But of course, I didn't have any illusions about becoming a photo-journalist. I didn't know if I had the ability and apart from that, further education is closed to Christians.

Much of my childhood and teenage years were spent amidst our local church. Chernogorsk has three Pentecostal churches. One registered and two nonregistered. We belonged to one of the nonregistered churches. Our church had about four hundred members, most of whom were young people. The Soviet government tried to create the illusion that the churches were attended mostly by old women—but that was merely an illusion.

I loved to hear the choirs sing. Siberian churches are noted for their beautiful singing. I can still hear some of those hymns ringing in my ears. It's one the loveliest sounds imaginable. In some churches, people would bring musical instruments to play—guitars, lutes, banjos, balalaikas, and all kinds of homemade stringed instruments, as well as trumpets, trombones, saxophones, and other brass instruments. When the full orchestra played, the hours would fly by, so wonderful was the sound of that majestic praise.

It was very difficult for our church to print Christian literature; many of the women would handcopy hymn books for use in church. Some of these books contained as many as five hundred hymns.

We had several services during the week, and each service could last four or five hours. We never did have an official church building, so the services would be held in people's homes, the rooms packed to the rafters with people. Usually the young men would be required to stand. Sometimes when the service continued for a very long time, our feet would ache. If the preacher were a dynamic speaker, we would quickly forget such things, but sometimes a dull speaker would be a forceful reminder of the cramped space. Despite the exhortations about heavenly rewards, we were often more aware of earthly discomforts.

In some churches in the USSR, Christians would meet at five in the morning to avoid detection, or late at night. Some meetings would be held outside in the woods or in some secret place. But in Chernogorsk the elders didn't want to be secretive, so the times of the services remained traditional. If the authorities complained about meetings in homes, it was quite usual to explain that someone in their midst was celebrating some special event or anniversary. Some quick-thinking young people would produce cake or treats as evidence. Churches in the Soviet Union regularly had many such "celebrations."

As I grew older, I came to share my parents' faith in our Lord Jesus Christ as my personal Lord and Savior. Over the weeks and months, I matured in my faith and found it incomprehensible that I should not be a Christian. Then I was willfully guilty of crimes against the state; I stood condemned by my faith.

I knew that my turn would come for attack. I too, would be faced with a choice. I did not have any illusions that I would be a daring warrior of faith, as bold as the many witnesses before me. But my confidence was in the Lord Jesus. Through Him, I would abide. If the days grew difficult, I knew His strength would increase. I claimed for my own this promise: "And your strength will equal your days."[14]

If we as a family had not had this steadfast assurance, our struggle would have been without end, and our strength would have failed. We would have been sinking in quicksand.

10

Secret Laws for Soviet Christians

"Here the Soviet government rules." The police had gone, but their words were ringing in our ears. At first no one moved.

And then life returned to our room. Surveying the damage around our home, my mother, sister, and aunt began clearing up, collecting the contents of drawers, and shelves, cupboards that had been strewn all over the floor.

Nadezhda walked into the back room to prepare tea for us and placed the old stone kettle on the stove. It seemed so early in the morning for a drink, but too late to go back to sleep. Besides, everyone has his own thoughts about the raid.

Recently raids had begun again on our home. They started shortly after my sixteenth birthday on April 30, 1978, and during May and June, they increased alarmingly. Police raids could last as long as two hours. The police could turn every corner of your home upside down, not caring about the damage they caused. At other times a raid would be over in ten minutes. The principal purpose of the raid was to scare, and usually it worked.

The morning after a police raid you are left with a strange feeling, something between fear and mystery. You may wonder how serious they are. How far have the investigations really gone? Do they really intend to arrest you, or is this only the local police chief's doing?

News travels fast in Chernogorsk. You walk down the street wondering if anyone is following you. People in the street stare at you. Do they know? Are they talking about you? It's not unusual for people to know where the police have been the night before. In the factory, the men lower their eyes as you enter the canteen. Many have experienced raids and know too much to joke about them. Women in shop windows whisper behind the counter. Across the street, the rumors spread behind curtains.

That day Nadezhda's tea tasted especially good because it warmed my insides. I love tea early in the morning, but usually not this early. Still, it cleared the mind. Together we began to review the situation. Was it true? Were the police really preparing a case against our whole family? What would happen to me if my parents, brothers, and aunt were imprisoned? I knew many families where the children had been "kidnapped" to be raised in state orphanages and indoctrinated with atheistic propaganda.

Someone in the room speculated that perhaps we would not be imprisoned. The threat of a police case was merely to scare us. We hoped we would get off with a heavy fine. No one really believed that, but we kept our deepest fears to ourselves. Fines, however, were serious enough. Many Christian leaders had been heavily fined. The pastor of our local church had been fined three times after police disrupted services. On one occasion, he had to pay as much as one hundred rubles in one month.

Could we avoid these clashes with the police by simply obeying the law? Clutching his mug of tea close to his cheek, the steam rising in front of his face, my father began to speak. "The problem can't be solved by simply observing the law and following the rules," he said. "Article 52 of the Soviet Constitution guarantees everyone the right and the freedom to profess any religion. The constitution guarantees our right to believe, but not the right to practice our faith. The Criminal Code of the Soviet Union is in direct contradiction with the Constitution. The Constitution gives you the right to believe. The Criminal Code gives the police the authority to arrest you if you practice your Christian faith.

"For Christians like us, things are even more difficult and complex. The Kremlin has instituted secret laws for dealing with believers; the KGB told me about them. These laws give them the authority to do anything they like with us. They can arrest us on false or completely fabricated charges."[15]

We talked at length of many people who had fought the system and won. Vladimir Bukovsky was one such person, who advocated the use of the law. He, himself, used the law brilliantly, at times completely tying up the Soviet machine in bureaucratic knots. This isn't usually possible, however, as it's very difficult to even find a copy of the Criminal Code or the constitution inside the USSR.

In his book *To Build a Castle,* Bukovsky says that the Soviets "wrote a constitution with a plethora of rights and freedoms which they simply cannot afford to grant, rightly supposing that nobody would be reckless enough to insist on them being observed."[16]

He suggested that citizens were obligated to observe the written law: "So let us defend our laws from being encroached upon by the authorities. *We* are on the side of the law. *They* are against it."[17]

The law is like an automobile. It can take you anywhere you want to go. All you need is a key to start up the engine. It's well-known that our country has close to full employment. Everyone has a job. Yet, ironically, some are arrested for parasitism. This is a familiar tactic of the KGB when dealing with dissidents and believers. First, they arrange to have you fired from your job. Then they make it difficult for you to get another job. That gives them the excuse to slap handcuffs on you for being a parasite of the state.

In 1965, the noted dissident and author Andrei Amalrik was sentenced to two and a half years exile for "parasitism." His book *Involuntary Exile into Siberia* deals with this subject at length.[18]

The Soviets are very clever. They are experts at propaganda. They show Western tourists the registered church in Moscow. The tour guide emphasizes the crowded church, and foreigners leave the country duly impressed. Of course, the tourists neglect to ask the tour guide how many churches there are in Moscow, a city of ten million people.[19]

How do ordinary people feel, and why don't they rise up against the regime? Oleg Bitov, the foreign culture editor of the *Literary Gazette,* who fled to England in October 1983, responded to this question in the *Sunday Telegraph:* "Such questions are excessively naive, for the people are controlled by very complicated processes, invisible to western observers. And because they are cut off from sources of free information by the Iron Curtain, their perception of the outside world is dangerously distorted."[20]

The Soviet Union is a desert island in a sea of news. Because of its large expanse and the censorship, it is difficult for a systematic and cohesive protest movement, such as the Solidarity Union in Poland, to emerge. Nevertheless, it is surprising to see the strength of the resistance. Not only is it widespread and spontaneous but also encompasses people from many walks of life. The publication of underground material and *samizdat* (self-publishing), such as *The Chronicle of Current Events*,[21] provides realistic pictures of a thriving resistance. The documentary evidence of the existing struggle is proof that resistance will never die.

I stepped outside and sat on a chair on the porch. The door was ajar, and I could hear the conversations inside. It was a clear night. The moonlight shone across the yard, and the stars were bright in the sky above. The chill of the night air ran through me, and my body gave a little shudder. In the moonlight I could see a cyclist approaching our home. As he passed by, he raised his arms and called out a greeting. Was he on his way to work at the bakery or was he returning home from the midnight shift at one of the factories? It was a tranquil scene. But inside the discussion continued fiercely and relentlessly.

"Communism is totally opposed to Christianity." I recognized the sound of Anatoly's voice. There was a murmur of general agreement, and then my Aunt Anna joined the debate.

"Communists fear the Christians. They hate them. Believers are their sworn enemies. They want to destroy all of us and our churches."

As I listened to their conversations from the porch, I felt like a sentry on night duty.

In the Communist world view, God is both an intruder

and an enemy. The objective of "the Cause" is to eradicate deep-rooted faith and belief that exists in a human heart. This attitude can be traced back to the original leaders of the movement.

In 1927, Stalin wrote:

> We are conducting and we will conduct a campaign against religious prejudices. The party cannot be neutral in relation to religion; it conducts a campaign against all religious prejudices of all kinds.[22]

Lenin's statements were just as explicit. In 1909, he wrote:

> It would be an error to confine the struggle against religion within an abstract ideological preaching, whereas we should rather tie this struggle to the concrete participation of the class movement aiming at making the social roots of religion disappear.[23]

Lenin also wrote:

> Religion and communism are incompatible in theory as well as in practice.[24]

> We must fight religion, this is the ABC of all Materialism and consequently of Marxism. But Marxism is not Materialism based on this ABC. Marxism goes further. It says: it is necessary to know how to fight religion and for this reason it is necessary to explain materialistically the source of faith and religion in the masses.[25]

> Marxism must be materialistic, that is to say the enemy of religion, but it is a dialectic materialism, that means that it places the struggle against religion not in an abstract manner on a theoretical and verbal field but concretely on the plane of the class struggle.[26]

Another Communist leader, Lounatcharski (Commissaire for Public Education) was even more direct. He wrote:

> We hate Christianity and the Christians. Even the best amongst them must be considered as our worst enemies. Down with love of our neighbors. What we need is hatred. We must learn to hate: this is the way in which we will conquer the world.[27]

The public image of the Soviet Union changes with time and is carefully and closely orchestrated. It is said that nothing happens by accident. The Kremlin still believes in the doctrine of hatred, but dressed in twentieth-century fashions, decorated in feathers of a dove, the assailant comes disguised as a man of peace. The strategy has changed; greater tolerance and acceptance is propagated. Only the gullible are fooled. We recognize the tactics.

In 1905, Lenin laid the ground rules:

> It is necessary that we are resolute in any sacrifice whatsoever, and even the need to practice everything possible: tricks, guiles, illegal methods; ready to suppress and conceal what is the truth; in short, it is in the interest of the struggle of the classes that we reduce our morals.
>
> It is necessary to learn the art of accepting political compromises, schemes, zigzags, maneuvers of conciliation and retreat, in short all the maneuvers necessary to accelerate the taking over of political power.[28]

I felt a movement behind me and turned to find my sister standing beside me with another cup of tea. "Thanks, Nadya," I said, "you must have been reading my mind."

Inside the conversation had stopped for a moment. No doubt, they, too, were also thankful for Nadezhda's refreshments and were taking a break. I knew exactly how everyone felt. Usually, I would have been among them, joining in the discussion. We didn't hate the Communists even though they hunted us like bandits; we prayed for them. Neither were we anti-Soviet. After all, we were sons and daughters of Siberia. If the Soviet government had not persecuted us, why would our family have wanted to leave the country? Siberia was our home.

I stood up and stretched. In the distance, the first rays of sunlight confirmed the coming of a warm, summer's day.

11

No Other Way

What would happen next? Would the police burst in and arrest us all or would they pick us up one at a time? What would happen to our family if the police case did proceed? This question dominated our thoughts.

On the day after the raid, we gathered together after the evening meal to discuss the events of recent days. During 1963, we had come to believe that God was calling our family to leave the Soviet Union. Since that time we had been trying to emigrate to a country where we could worship God freely and where our children would enjoy that freedom in the future. We had written hundreds of pages of appeals to the Soviet authorities and the Kremlin, also to Christians in the West requesting their help. In accordance with Soviet law, we had taken the first step in the emigration process, rejecting our Soviet citizenship.

We were not requesting special privileges. Emigration

was our right. Article 13(2) of the Universal Declaration of Human Rights, adopted by the United Nations in 1948, states simply:

> Everyone has the right to leave any country including his own and to return to his country.

But the Soviet government refuses to keep the laws they have instituted (the Soviet Constitution) and the international laws that they have signed (Helsinki Final Act: see Appendix) and promised to uphold.[29]

To leave the Soviet Union, two things are required: first, an invitation from abroad, preferably by a blood relative permitting "family reunification;" secondly, an exit visa from the OVIR (Emigration and Visa Office) issued by the Soviet authorities.

The first step in getting an exit visa is to receive an invitation, although this guarantees nothing.

Since we had no relatives in the West, we had no invitation. Consequently, we had little hope of getting an exit visa.

Late at night, we would listen to radio broadcasts from the West. Although the Soviet government spends millions of rubles jamming such broadcasts, people inside the USSR can still pick up some of the stations. Most people understand that the broadcasts are one of the best sources of factual information about world events as well as daily USSR events. For many people in the Soviet Union, they are a tremendous source of encouragement. For us, in June 1978, they represented a dim flicker of light.

From the Voice of America, we understood that America worked for the rights of people all over the world. America, we were told, was the defender of justice in the free world and would support victims of injustice—people like us.

That night our conversation changed direction. We began to wonder how we could communicate with Christians in America, tell them about the problems facing our family, and plead with them for help.

After a few days, we decided that we must visit the American Embassy in Moscow. Surely, someone would take pity on us and help. God would find a way of touching someone's heart. For the first time we felt hopeful.

I was convinced and encouraged the plan. Unanimously, our family agreed that Mama would go to Moscow. At first, one of my brothers had planned to travel with my mother. And then the plan changed. It was decided that I would go. I was sixteen and could be confiscated by the authorities, in the event of my parents' arrest. I could be forced into a reeducation institute. Also as soon as I passed the legal age of consent, the authorities could force me to serve in the army. This was against my conscience, and like many other Christians, I would refuse to obey, even though the consequences were three years in a labor camp. Thus, it made sense for me to travel with Mama to Moscow.

Moscow.

The word filled me with dread, yet I felt a strange tingling inside. I was convinced that the answer to our problem lay beyond Chernogorsk. In an inexplicable way, Moscow played a part in our lives. Yet if the local police in Chernogorsk had not threatened five members of our family with imprisonment, we would never have gone.

My mother decided to travel to Moscow with the Vashchenkos, close family friends who lived on our street in Chernogorsk.

Both Peter and Augustina Vashchenko had suffered severely for their faith. Both had been imprisoned, and even at that time, their eldest son Alexander was serving a three-year sentence for refusing to serve in the Soviet Army. They decided to travel to Moscow with their three eldest daughters Lidiya, Lyuba, and Lilya and their seventeen-year-old son John.

Unlike us, the Vashchenkos had already received an invitation from abroad.[30]

The night the decision to leave for Moscow was finally made I could hardly sleep. I knew there was a tremendous risk involved. But I also knew that there was no other way.

MOSCOW

1

Incident at the Gates

It was the first clear day in a long time. Moscow's weather had been cold and rainy. June was generally a warm and sunny month, but summer was late this year. That day, however, it was warm. You could look up and see miles and miles of clear blue sky.

The six-thousand-kilometer journey from Chernogorsk took three-and-a-half days by train. During the long trip many questions raced through my mind as we passed through picturesque countryside and speeded by small towns and villages where young children ran alongside the track and waved to the conductor. What would happen when we reached Moscow? Would we be arrested by the KGB and thrown into an anonymous prison somewhere? Would we find a way of sending a message to Christians in the West? I had no doubt that if the KGB caught our little group we would be arrested. We would have to be careful not to attract their attention. I knew that the KGB had only one answer for all our questions.

The main railway terminal at Moscow's central station was busy, bustling with energy. People were rushing to board trains, leaving the capital. Undoubtedly, others were, like me, on their first visit to Moscow. I was too anxious about the events that lay ahead to eat or drink anything, and no one else in our group wanted to stop for breakfast either. We didn't talk a lot. There was little to say.

We went directly to the subway station. I was impressed with the efficient system, an underground network connecting all regions of the city with its center. The subways themselves were huge, impressive, ornate structures. The escalators that transported us into the bowels of the earth seemed endlessly long. We decided it would be safer to walk part of the way to the embassy, so we left the subway one stop before the one nearest the embassy so the KGB wouldn't spot us. Peter and Augustina Vashchenko and John walked in front, followed closely by Lidiya, Lyuba, and Lilya. Mama walked behind, and I, being the youngest, was last.

No one knew what would happen. Although the United States and the USSR have signed a Consular Convention guaranteeing "free access" to the Consul Section, in practice it is considered a crime to spend more than three hours inside a foreign embassy. Soviet militia patrol outside the gates of foreign embassies, and usually visitors have to produce passports on entry. Soviet people are frequently detained and forbidden access. It was well-known that there had been many incidents outside the gates of the embassies. Many people had been assaulted by the Soviet militia while trying to enter the buildings. Even

Peter and Augustina Vashchenko had been assaulted outside the gates of the American Embassy.

As we walked along Chaikovskovo Street, one of Moscow's busy ring roads, I could see the embassy in the distance. It was a large ochre-colored building with ten floors. Over two hundred Americans worked there. I was surprised to learn later that as many as two hundred Soviets were also employed as translators, secretaries, drivers, and cleaners.

I noticed two entrances to the building itself, large arches wide enough for cars to drive through. Two Soviet militia were on duty outside. We approached them and asked if we could enter the embassy. They refused.

Suddenly, John Vashchenko tried to rush through the archway. But the militia men moved just as swiftly. Both the militia men grabbed John and threw him to the ground. This left the gates unguarded. Without thinking we ran into the courtyard at the back of the building. I followed the others, moving just as quickly, not wanting to be caught. My last glimpse of John was his being punched by the guard.

One of the first persons I saw in the courtyard was the U.S. Consul. Anxiously we tried to explain what had happened to John outside and the reason for our visit. The consul tried to calm us. He invited us into the embassy and led us through the side entrance away from the main gates. Silently we followed. Walking briskly, I barely had time to observe the different rooms and hallways we passed through to a large reception area, the consul's waiting room.

On the wall facing us was a large, framed, color photograph of the President of the United States: the smiling face of Jimmy Carter peered down on us. The office appeared busy as other visitors crowded around a desk. A consul staff member tried to answer questions, and the inquirers were then handed forms to complete. Behind partitions I could detect the smoky reflection of people, a small office at work.

Peter Vashchenko sounded anxious. In staccato sentences he explained the incident outside the gates. His hands moved jerkily. The expressions on our faces revealed our fright. Would the consul help by finding out about John, and could he join us?

To my surprise, the American diplomat didn't appear to share our concern about John's fate.

He pointed out that this was an internal Soviet matter and out of his jurisdiction. He said he could not complain to the police about their handling of a Soviet citizen. Our relief at reaching the safety of the embassy's shelter was quickly turning to alarm. As each minute ticked away, the chances of rescuing John from outside the embassy were decreasing.

I stared at the consul in puzzlement and helplessness. Didn't he understand the dangers? Why couldn't he respond to our plea for John? Embassy staff had helped people in similar circumstances. An hour passed. Two things were clear: John had disappeared; the embassy would offer no help.

The consul listened to us as we repeated the reasons for our visit to Moscow. Again he shook his head. He was sorry, but there was nothing he could do. Now he must get back to work. There were some urgent matters on his desk. Our impromptu meeting was at an end. We would have to leave.

We listened to his words with bitter disappointment. If the embassy couldn't help us, where could we turn? We had pinned all our hopes on this trip to Moscow. And our thoughts kept returning to John. Where was he now? Once again we asked if the embassy could establish his whereabouts and secure his safe return to us. We said that if John were rescued, we would leave.

The consul discussed this with us for some time. He expressed his regret and repeated he could not help us. Again he advised us to leave. Then excusing himself politely, he returned to his office behind the partitions. For the consul staff, it was business as usual.

We stayed in the waiting room, unsure what to do. Should we return to Chernogorsk immediately or stay in Moscow in the hope of finding John? Where could we begin looking? If we went to the Soviet authorities, we would have to explain the reasons for our visit to the American Embassy, and having visited the embassy, why we had stayed. As each hour passed, the dangers increased. We were caught with our backs to the wall. Whatever decision we made, the path led to an interrogation cell with the KGB. All our thoughts were with John and with our family back home. We went round and round in circles. What could we do? We couldn't fight the KGB. We knew that John could be lost, like many others, in the labyrinth of the KGB's nether world. Our only hope of rescuing him was through the influence of the American Embassy.

From time to time, the consul or one of his aides emerged to check something in another office. They seemed dismayed to find that we were still in the waiting room. A tall, thin man with horn-rimmed spectacles walked in, moving in sharp, awkward motions. Trying to avoid someone else who had entered the room through another door, he stumbled and fell over a chair. It was an amusing scene, but at that moment, I could see nothing funny. I had almost forgotten how to laugh.

The light in the reception area was growing dim. All at once I realized just how long we had been waiting in the embassy. We had nowhere to go with night coming on. From the corner of my eye, I saw someone from the consul's office move toward the main exit and press a switch. In an instant the reception was ablaze with neon brightness. I squinted slightly as I adjusted to the light in the room.

For several hours no one had spoken to us. It was evident that the embassy staff was ignoring us. Perhaps they thought by doing this they could get us to leave. Two women walked out of the consul's office carrying their handbags and discussing plans for the evening. They chatted together as they walked to the exit. One by one the consul's staff left, and the lights in the inner office went out. Business was over for another day.

I glanced around the office. The night seemed cold and unfriendly. We had not eaten all day, and I felt faint from hunger. We realized that the sanctity of diplomatic soil offered us some protection. The KGB couldn't reach us as long as we stayed inside the embassy. But we were balancing precariously at the edge of a steep cliff. If the earth moved with the slightest tremor, we would be lost. I tried to relax on the sofas in the waiting room. How long could we remain here? Would the Americans force us to leave?

Simas Kudirka.

The words appeared in my mind from nowhere, a ghost from the past returning to haunt me. In October 1970, Simas Kudirka, a forty-year-old Lithuanian radio operator, jumped from a Soviet fishing trawler to an American coast guard ship, the *Vigilant*. While still in U.S. waters, Soviet seamen boarded the American vessel and demanded his return.

"I put up as good a fight as I could, but six sailors wrestled me down," he was to say later.

At his trial, he was accused of the crime of wanting to leave the country, and he was sentenced to ten years in prison.

We were in a very unusual situation. We had not planned to stay, but we felt we couldn't leave. The embassy had tried to put pressure on us to leave, to push us out, but they hadn't actually taken us by force and placed us at the gates. We prayed together, committing the days ahead to God. Only He knew what was to come.

There was a small toilet with a wash basin, which we could use, and the light in the reception area remained on all night. The clock on the far wall silently recorded the passing of time. I was restless and slept little.

2

Camping in the Reception Area

I looked at the calendar on the wall with its panoramic view of the Grand Canyon. It was June 28. Twenty-four hours had passed. It was our second day in Moscow, and I had seen nothing of the city. Quietly we waited in one corner of the reception area.

None of us could predict what would happen. Next week seemed far away. I could not even think about the day ahead, but worried about the next few moments.

All around us the normal routine of an office and of consular life continued. Sometimes there was a flurry of activity. Secretaries walked briskly with letters to be signed and documents to be photocopied; they hurried to answer telephones. At other times the pace slowed, and coffee breaks always meant a chat in the corridor. We watched all this silently. Those in the office carried on with their routines as though we didn't exist.

Time passed slowly. Still we continued to sit in one corner of the reception area of the Consul Section. Just as we had thought we had no friends, some kind people took pity on us and secretly brought us food.

When the embassy officials saw that we were determined to stay, despite the difficulties, they decided to begin inquiries about John. The Soviet response was, "John? John who? Never heard of him." Of course it was no surprise to us that the Soviet authorities claimed to have no information about the incident outside the embassy gates on June 27 and that they could give the Americans no advice or suggestions. Eventually, however, the Soviet Foreign Ministry did confirm that John Vashchenko had been returned home to Siberia under police escort. Could that be true?

Peter Vashchenko almost managed a smile, as he confirmed that the embassy had agreed to help them contact their children in Chernogorsk. On July 6, the embassy sent a telegram to the Chernogorsk Post Office in the name of Vera Vashchenko. Since Alexander was still in a medium-regime labor camp in the mountains east of Krasnoyarsk, Vera, aged twenty-two, was the oldest daughter living in the Vashchenko home.

The Vashchenkos kept expecting to hear from Vera, and as the days passed, their relief at John's alleged return turned to alarm. Why hadn't Vera communicated with her parents? What was going on back in Chernogorsk? Then after four days, the Vashchenko family was able to speak to Vera on the telephone. Explaining the reason for her silence, Vera told them that she had been chased out of the post office and couldn't get to a telephone until then.

Vera confirmed that John was safe at home. But he had been tortured "almost to the point of death" and was in such pain he could not walk to the post office to talk with his parents. They were to write later. Vera advised the Vashchenkos to stay in the embassy until some assurances could be given. When we finally spoke to our family, we were encouraged to do the same. *Stay in the embassy.*

If they could torture a minor so severely, what would they do to us? Chernogorsk was six thousand kilometers from Moscow, and even if we were allowed to return home, what hope did we have of communicating with anyone in the West? Would we ever be allowed to return to Moscow?

This time our decision to remain was not a difficult one for us. But for the embassy officials, the dilemma increased. On virtually every contact with American officials, we were told that we must leave.

To some people we must have seemed like ignorant peasants, simple people who had misunderstood and overestimated the power of the Americans. But we understood only too well that the American diplomats were anxious to avoid a confrontation with the Soviets—not over people like us. We were not famous dissidents, celebrated scientists, human rights activists, intellectuals, writers, or politicians. We were two ordinary Christian families.

The situation could have been resolved easily. All we would have had to do was walk out of the consul's waiting room. The American diplomats could probably foresee the complications of letting us stay. Yet we knew equally well the consequences of leaving. Our act was unprecedented. In Soviet eyes, we were guilty of a serious offense. Usually Soviet citizens were punished severely if they stayed longer than three hours in a foreign embassy. And we had lived on American soil for over thirty days! Our crime would not be forgiven. An example would have to be made of us, to deter others. Then the situation was complicated further when an Armenian woman, whose mother had emigrated to California, dashed past police guards with her two small boys and joined us.[31]

I tried to stay as silent and as still as I could during the day while the consul staff were at work. At times my bones would ache from not moving. The stiffness turned to numbness, and I could barely move my limbs when I tried to walk at night after the office had closed. Even worse, one month had passed since we had left Chernogorsk and had had our last shower and bath. At night we tried to clean the divans and us with damp rags but we now felt humiliated.

Some staff members showed their clear displeasure at our squalor by holding a handkerchief to their noses when passing us. Some walked by with contemptuous glances barely disguising their hostility and disgust. They did not understand that our fate hung by a thread. Thirty-four days after we entered the embassy, we were permitted our first bath; we were allowed showers each week thereafter.

On July 27, one of the senior staff at the embassy called on Kornienko, the Soviet foreign minister, who confirmed that we needed an invitation from a blood relative who lived abroad before the Soviet government would issue an exit visa. But none of our family had anyone who lived abroad or who had received permission to emigrate. The door was firmly closed.

Not everyone ignored us. A few Christians in the embassy befriended us. The vice-consul gave us a Bible we took turns reading. I read the Bible from cover to cover during those few weeks. It became our most valuable possession. He sent a telegram to Pastor Williamson in

Alabama, the man whose church had sponsored the Vashchenko family. Christian friends continued to help us sometimes against the wishes of the embassy, by bringing us food at night and toilet items that we needed. And through correspondents, such as David Willis of the *Christian Science Monitor,* a few news items were published in the international press.

One day a silver-haired, dignified man entered the consul office and noticed us sitting silently in the corner of the room. Unlike the others, he walked across and inquired who we were and what we were doing there. "I will try to help you," he said. "I will write to Mr. Brezhnev and ask him to give you exit visas. I will emphasize your rights according to the Helsinki Final Act, which he himself signed in 1975. Don't hold out too much hope, though, because Brezhnev never replies to any of my letters these days. It's a difficult situation, but don't give up hope. If I can help you, I will."

The man was Dr. Andrei Sakharov. I felt very proud to have met such a famous man and very encouraged that he had taken the trouble to inquire into our problem. He took time to talk with us. No one can imagine what that meant to us. Later we learned from his wife, Yelena Bonner, that he had written two letters to Brezhnev for us but never received any reply.

I knew that the Soviet militia were still patrolling outside the gates of the embassy. There were more policemen in a booth just around the corner from the embassy. Someone said that there were KGB cars outside the gates waiting to take us away. Every time I closed my eyes, a picture of the police sergeant in Chernogorsk came to mind. His face haunted me—I remembered him staring directly at me and asking my parents what would become of me if they were both arrested.

3

Depart!

Life seemed a puzzle. Why had this happened to us? We hadn't wanted it to happen. Why wouldn't the Americans try to help us? The more I thought about it, the more questions I had. All day long we waited in the corner, like naughty school children about to be punished.

Two months went by. We were still in the reception area, ignored and isolated.

We composed a joint letter of appeal addressed to President Carter and gave it to a tourist who was visiting the U.S. Consul. He agreed to carry the letter out of the Soviet Union and to mail it when he reached America. President Carter was a powerful man. He was also a Christian. Could he respond to his Christian brothers and sisters who needed his help?

When the embassy officials realized that we had written directly to President Carter they were furious. Seeking a quick solution, the embassy increased the pressure.

On August 26 came the moment we feared most. That evening one of the American couples who had befriended us was sitting talking with us. I was leaning against the back of one of the divans listening when the door to the reception area opened and a marine guard entered. He strode over toward us but without looking at us addressed the Americans. "Why are you here? Don't you know you're not allowed to talk to these people?" He then said, "I think you'd better leave." Reluctantly, the couple departed.

Something was happening, and I was scared. I looked at the clock on the far wall. It was a quarter past eight. About fifteen minutes later, the door opened again. This time the U.S. political officer and the consul entered. We all stood to our feet.

"We received instructions from Washington about your case," the political officer spoke calmly but decisively. He held some papers in his right hand, and choosing one of them, he raised it toward the light and began to read the statement. It said that our presence in the embassy hindered the emigration of believers and was not helping our own case. The ambassador, he read, had thought us to be honest people, but we had turned out not to be because we would not go. We could no longer remain in the embassy and must leave immediately "with God." The officer made a reassuring gesture with his other arm encouraging us to move. "I'll accompany you to the gates," he said.

I could feel my heart begin to beat faster. My mouth was dry; I tried to speak but I could make no sound. Repeatedly we had been told by the Soviet authorities, "The Americans don't want you." Now, it seemed, we were face to face with the facts. I knew what lay beyond the gates. The KGB would help us with transport and an escort. But where would that lead? I didn't look at anyone else. I felt my body begin to shake; I was very frightened. I never thought that the people with whom we had sought shelter would become the ones to hand us over to greater danger.

"We will not walk out of the embassy. If you want us to leave, you will have to order the marines to carry us out and hand us over to the KGB."

The silence was deafening. I could feel my heart still pounding wildly. I rested my hands on the divan to steady myself. I felt as though all my worst fears and nightmares had been unleashed simultaneously. I could scarcely believe the scene before me. The two Americans exchanged glances. Were they about to call the guards?

After what seemed like hours but in reality only a minute or so, the two men withdrew. We sank down on the divans in relief. No one spoke.

The next day we remained silent as consulate life continued uninterrupted. But when evening came, we spoke quietly among ourselves, trying to predict the next move. President Carter hadn't replied directly to us, but he did communicate to the embassy, instructing them not to evict us by force, but to encourage us to leave voluntarily. If President Carter had not communicated with the embassy, I reasoned that Moscow officials would eventually force us to leave. As it was, they could put still more pressure on us to leave. That evening as we were talking, the officials came with the same command, loud and clear: *depart!* And again we refused.

I felt that things could not continue like this much longer. We had reached a climax, and something was bound to happen. Have you ever lit a match and held it in front of you? The heat from the flame can warm you on a cool evening. It can also singe your fingers. It's a matter of time until the flame burns its way through the tiny matchstick. We had seen the flame. Very soon we would feel the fire.

For two months we had stayed awake late and risen early. We were edgy and tense, wondering what each day would bring. When the danger was so intense, the risks so great, and the insults almost too much to bear, the pages of the Bible became our one source of hope.

For the third night in succession, the American officials returned. This time they asked us to collect together our meager belongings and go with them. Silently we followed, uncertain of our fate. The diplomat took us through several rooms and hallways, down some stairs, and along another corridor. Soon we found ourselves on the other side of the building. I didn't know where we were going but I did know two exits of the embassy, and this didn't seem to be leading there. Was there another entrance that we knew nothing about?

The trail led through yet another corridor and finally into a little room in the basement, which we later found out, had been used in the past by marine messengers who stayed overnight. It had two beds, a small table, and an upright chair. A few smaller chairs were placed near one wall beside a stove and a refrigerator. One corner of the room had a sink and a tap. The room had a tiny barred window overlooking Chaikovskovo Street where the Soviet militia patrolled. It was the only view of the world outside. I had no idea that this was to be our home for the next few years.

4

Basement Refuge

It was difficult to comprehend that sixty-four days had passed since we entered the American Embassy to ask for help. From June until August, we had lived in the reception area. Our hopes had been high when we approached the embassy building. We felt sure that someone would take pity and help us. Now, it seemed, we were struggling to survive. What was to become of us? In the reception area, we at least met visitors to the embassy. Mail arrived for the foreign correspondents at the embassy, and frequently they visited the consul section. Then we had opportunity to talk to some of the journalists in Moscow, and as a result, some small news items about our plight appeared in the Western press. It was suggested that perhaps the embassy had moved us to prevent our talking freely to visitors and correspondents.

I don't know if anyone slept that first night in the

basement. We knelt on the cold basement floor and thanked God for safety and protection.

The next day passed slowly. The room was clean but cramped. It was hard to move around without bumping into someone. Mama sat on one of the beds by the far wall, and I sat beside her. Peter and Augustina Vashchenko sat opposite with Lidiya. Lyuba and Lilya sat on chairs close-by. The Vashchenko family talked among themselves, leaving Mama and I to discuss these new developments. I wondered how long we would have to stay here. We all spoke in hushed whispers because no one was sure who would be listening to our conversations.

"Guess who's the first to know that we've moved from the reception area?" Lidiya asked. We followed her gaze. Outside the metal grille of the window frame, the Soviet militia guard peered into the basement room.

Lilya moved to the entrance of the room as we continued to debate recent events. Suddenly she motioned us to silence. "Someone's coming," she said softly. We stood on our feet as an embassy official entered the room. I couldn't imagine what he was going to say. Being the youngest in the group, I remained silent. The man from the embassy was courteous but businesslike. He suggested that we should seriously reconsider leaving the embassy. In the meantime, we had been allocated temporary accommodation: we would be permitted to remain in this basement room. I looked around the room as he spoke. I couldn't imagine living in this room. And for how long?

He told us that we would be permitted to leave the room if accompanied by someone from the consul's office, otherwise movement would be limited. Our room was considered a "restricted area," and contact with diplomats, tourists, and visitors was not allowed. A "limited access" list was issued, initially to members of just five families. This meant that a few of the embassy personnel would be able to visit us in the basement. Food would be provided by the embassy from a "refugee budget." The rules were simple, the instructions uncomplicated. This message delivered, the messenger retreated to the consul's territory.

No one could think of anything to say. We each remained where we were for several minutes. I walked to the sink and opened a small cupboard above it. Inside were a few glasses. Taking one out, I rinsed it under the tap and filled it to the brim, gulping the water. Now that we had been moved, what was to become of us? How many times I had already asked myself that question!

"Where are we?" one of the Vashchenko girls asked aloud. We had been moved at night and were unsure of our immediate location. One by one we emerged from our shelter to explore our surroundings. Our room was at the end of a hallway. Immediately adjacent to us was a toilet and a shower and next door a barber shop for embassy employees, attended by a Soviet lady.

I walked down the narrow, winding corridor that widened immediately below a staircase. In front was another door leading to the embassy courtyard, the archway, and the Soviet militia. At the other end, the corridor led down a few steps into an open area that housed a large, noisy power generator. At the far end, I noticed a repair shop where another Soviet employee sat at a desk. I was told he repaired electronic equipment.

The passageway led on toward the end of the embassy building, past several padlocked rooms.

We settled down to life in the basement room, but things were still tense and edgy. I lived with the thought of being evicted. Whenever I heard footsteps down the corridor, whenever an official entered the room, I feared the time had come when we would be forcibly turned out. I dreaded that it would happen at night. As day followed day, however, I slowly recovered. It seemed that we had been buried alive and virtually forgotten. The basement room had to be our living room, dining room, kitchen, and bedroom. The little window gave us our only glimpse of the outside world.

The courtyard at the rear of the embassy was somber. One day during that first week I noticed several Soviet drivers leaning against a black embassy sedan. They were smoking American cigarettes and staring directly at me. For one moment an image flashed across my mind; I saw myself being kidnapped: a hood pushed over my face, my arms twisted behind my back, bundled into the back seat of an unmarked car, and driven out of the embassy. As quickly as the image had come, it faded. But I didn't linger by the cars and carefully stayed close to the Americans who escorted us on our daily walks.

We were generally allowed out for about an hour or two each day. This time passed quickly, and all too soon we had to return to the basement. The area by the far wall of the embassy building was referred to as the playground, a sandy patch with a swing, some planks of wood, some other toys, and a small tree. After spending our day indoors watching a blank wall, even this patch of earth was welcome. On our walk we also passed a coffeehouse where we could see embassy staff sitting and chatting on weekdays and worshiping in church services on Sunday.

I was curious about Western church services. How did the services differ from Soviet ones? Could they possibly be any longer? Quietly I was told that permission had not been received for us to attend.

On our first Sunday I sat in our basement when the service began and read from the Scriptures. I turned the pages of the Bible we had been given and silently read from Matthew 18:20: "For where two or three are gathered together in My name there am I in the midst of them."

One day during our hour outside in the courtyard, I noticed laborers on a construction site immediately behind the playground area. Later I was told that a new building was under construction to house the American Embassy. The inevitable question that we pondered was: What would happen to us if the embassy moved?

5

The First Christmas

Moscow pavements can be very slippery in winter. I had to smile as an icy patch on the street tripped up yet another pedestrian. None of us had anticipated such a long stay in the embassy. Because it was summer when we arrived in Moscow, we were all wearing light clothes. Now I was sitting huddled in one corner, when the message came: A visitor had arrived to see us.

Snow was falling as one by one we ventured outside into the cold. I walked briskly to the rear of the courtyard, my hands deep in my pockets. In the playground I shook hands with our visitor, the Reverend John Pollock from England.

John Pollock had first visited the Soviet Union in 1963, shortly after the demonstration of the "Thirty-two Christians from Siberia" at the American Embassy in Moscow. He had received a commission from a British and American publisher to find out more about these people, about

Christian life, and any expression of its survival. Although he had been unable to meet anyone from Chernogorsk, his book *The Christians from Siberia* concluded with a chapter on the protest at the embassy. That book was the first publication to deal with evangelical Christianity in the Soviet Union after nearly half a century of militant atheistic rule.[32]

Paul and Annette Rousch, a Christian couple working in the embassy, happened to be reading Pollock's book at the time of our entry in June. They contacted the author, living in Devon, England, and arranged our encounter.

As we talked, I brushed off the snowflakes that gathered in my hair. There was much to say, but not enough time. And I felt inadequate trying to put our experiences into words. Snow began to fall even more heavily, and I could feel the cold right through my bones. My Siberian shoes were sturdy, but they had been made for Siberian roads not for winter in Moscow.

Back in the basement we tried to warm ourselves. As a result of such "outings," we were frequently ill. That winter, each time we had a visitor, we caught a cold. Nevertheless, it seemed a small price to pay for hopeful news and a friendly face. John Pollock's visit encouraged me. Despite the cold, I felt the warmth of his sincere desire to help us.

When he first arrived in Moscow, his intention had been to write a short, imaginative version of his impressions. But after our meeting, it was decided that we would each write an account of our lives. The publication of such a volume, it was hoped, would persuade the Soviet authorities to grant us exit visas.

With the help of Christians in Moscow, including the Rouschs and Kent Hill, a young American graduate doing research for a doctorate in Russian history, a network was set up. The following weeks were spent writing about our life and experiences in Siberia. As our stay in the embassy lengthened, so did our writings. With the help of these friends, they were translated and passed on to John Pollock in England.

Six months had passed since we left Chernogorsk. No one could have known that things would have turned out this way, but then who can predict the future? After living like criminals in Siberia, we did not expect to become fugitives inside the American Embassy.

It was difficult to adjust to the day-to-day routine of life in the basement. The psychological pressures were intense. We were from two different families, living in close, cramped quarters, separated from our families at home, and feeling cut off from the rest of the world. Our Christian friends in the embassy tried to encourage us and lift our spirits, but many days we were filled with a kind of foreboding and uncertainty.

For me, things were awkward because I was the only boy and much younger than Lidiya, Lyuba, and Lilya, although we were friends. During the few hours we spent outside, I would watch some of the young American boys in the embassy and long to be able to play with them. Sometimes Peter and I would exercise together or pretend to kick a ball around. As we ventured out each day for our "walkabouts" and exercise, the Moscow winter seemed quite severe. All around us embassy staff were preparing for Christmas: Cards and gifts were exchanged; carols and hymns were sung; special services were arranged at the chapel, all to celebrate the birth of Jesus.

At such times, even those who were unbelievers joined in the festivities, exchanging presents and greetings. The offices were decorated with colored papers and balloons. Some of the diplomats' children were excited, counting the days before they were free to open their presents, carefully wrapped beneath their finely decorated trees. It seemed to us that Santa Claus was the only visitor who didn't need an entry or exit visa.

Christmas is not a holiday in the USSR. If it falls on a weekday, everyone is expected to work. For believers it's a family occasion, but for many who are separated from loved ones in prison or in the camps the festivities are tinged with sadness. This Christmas we decided to observe a fast.

We held a simple service in the basement. We sang hymns and special Christmas songs. We read the Scriptures and shared our thoughts with one another. Mama missed the family gatherings we used to enjoy, especially since Vladimir and his wife Katherina had recently become parents (Roman was born on July 29). So Mama was a grandmother, but she hadn't seen her grandchild. Her tears expressed the feelings of an aching heart. Augustina Vashchenko also missed her children, especially her eight-year-old Sarah and four-year-old Abraham. They were always in her thoughts and prayers. For me at sixteen, this was my first Christmas away from Chernogorsk and a lonely time. All my thoughts were of a small, wooden house, deep in the heart of Siberia. Yet, despite the pain of separation, we were comforted as our hearts reached out to each other across the miles and were united in prayer.

On that first Christmas when we were still on the embassy's restricted list, we were allowed no Christmas visitors.

After Christmas we spent a lot of time writing down our experiences for John Pollock. I would sit on a chair by the window wondering what I could write. Did Christians in the West really want to know about me? What could I tell them? Washington—London—Paris seemed far, far away. I found myself thinking back over my life. Many incidents came to mind: my father's arrest; stories from Aunt Anna's experiences in exile—how was she, I wondered; visiting Papa in camp; night raids on our home in Chernogorsk; and testimony from Christian brothers and sisters who had been arrested and imprisoned.

Alone, with few people to talk to or to play with, I spent my time reading the Bible. How strange it must have been to have lived at the time of Jesus. Some saw Him in the marketplace, in the temple, and on the hilltop. They knew Him, but they didn't recognize Him as the "Son of God." To many people, He was just another radical underground leader. I read the Gospels again and again. I imagined what Jesus was like. He had time for everyone and never turned anyone away. He was direct, confident, assured, yet sensitive. At times, He must have seemed like a shaman, who spoke in puzzling images and did conjuring tricks. What if Jesus were here in person? How would He handle this situation?

I had come here a playful and energetic boy. I had had my own ideas of life and plans for the future. One single incident had changed everything. Now I was almost a prisoner, feeling like a captive. At times, it seemed as though my life was not my own. I wanted to rebel, to shout out that I was too young to be caught up in this complex situation. Why wouldn't people help us?

Gradually I came to accept the fact that I had to forget youthful pursuits and ambitions. I had to face responsibility and live my life. In my land, many believers were being tortured for their faith. I must find a way to help them. But

I had no control over what was happening. My fate was in another's hands. How could I be a follower of Jesus here in this basement?

With the passing of time, I felt a movement within myself. I was becoming a man. I picked up my pen and found myself writing a poem. I imagined that I was addressing Christians in foreign lands and dedicated it to all the martyrs in the USSR and other Communist countries. I never thought anyone would read it, keeping it secretly in my notebook. Some time later I entitled the poem "On the Defense!"

On the Defense!

Think about your loved ones.
About: how people are dying here.
About: how Christians are mocked.
About: how many are in insane asylums.

I beg you to think of those—
of those who are already considered dead;
who are heavily drugged in psychiatric hospitals;
of those who are dying in prisons and labor camps.

As I ask all of you,
my dear friends,
all of my dear brothers and sisters in Christ,
think of them and make your decision.

Thus they await God's help,
thus they thirst after righteousness.
How they would like to be
the masters of their own destiny,
to live free in their own country.

But God wants you to work,
to be fully dedicated to godly pursuits,
And to intercede on their behalf,—
those in psychiatric hospitals, prisons,

labor camps and in exile.

May they be allowed to live in peace,
either in this country or in some other,
for those hoping for permission to emigrate
to a country in which they want to live
so they can worship God there in freedom.

6

Laughter at Midnight

I heard the noise but I didn't know what it was. It was an eerie, sinister sound and had awakened me from a heavy sleep. It had a metallic tone and seemed to be coming from the window. From my makeshift bed on the floor of the basement, I stared outside. I could see nothing, just the bleak Moscow night, deserted streets, barred windows, doors bolted. There was a strange stillness disturbed only by the footsteps of the Soviet militia guards, patrolling the gates outside. I closed my eyes and tried to sleep.

Rattle.

There it was again, a noise by the window.

The burly figure of a Soviet guard blocked my view. His frame filled the window. For an instant, our eyes met. He appeared to be grinning. In his hand he held a nightstick. Looking directly at me, he slowly trailed this along the metal grating outside the window.

Rattle! Rattle! Rattle!

The noise sent a chill through me. It was more frightening than mere threats and curses because it didn't sound human. It defined our role as captives. Now I knew how animals in a zoo felt. For children it is a thrill to take a stick and rattle the lion's cage. How pleasing to see the great beast of the jungle stalk from side to side, pacing the length and breadth of its confinement.

The militia man walked on down Chaikovskovo Street. I lay on my bed listening to his footsteps fading slowly into the night. Sleep wouldn't come, and each time I heard footsteps, my eyes froze at the window. The footsteps stopped at our window. He paused, glanced in, and then walked on. An hour later, the rattle returned.

We complained about the noise at the window, and the embassy passed on our complaints to the militia. The rattling at night stopped—for a while, but the militia found other imaginative ways to disturb our sleep as they whistled, talked loudly, and cursed outside the window. Like all Soviet workers they got paid every two weeks, and sometimes they would get drunk after receiving their wages. We knew we could always expect a troublesome night on payday. Sometimes they would walk by shouting at each other and cursing blasphemously. Some would mimic a dog or a cat. Sometimes the threats were meant directly for us. "Very soon you'll be in our hands, then we'll do anything we want." The threats went into explicit detail.

"Don't worry, we've got time. We can wait," they would shout into our room. "We'll always be here. We're not going anywhere."

Some of the Soviet employees at the embassy would taunt us with veiled threats and jokes. "There go our emigrants." They would laugh as we walked past. Once I found the crushed body of my pet kitten who had died under the wheels of an embassy car with a Soviet driver at the wheel.

To emphasize our situation, one news report described our basement as a "dungeon." Of course, this was an exaggeration. Neither were we in a prison cell, although sometimes that was what it felt like. I could have walked out of the basement at any time I chose. The consequences of such action were obvious, but I was free to make that decision. The basement was not a prison cell, and we were not prisoners. Perhaps a more apt description is that we were "hostages of conscience." The dangers were, nonetheless, very real.

I was at our little wooden table in the basement writing a letter home on March 28, 1979, when I became aware of something happening outside the window. The militia men were running from one side to the other, talking loudly and quickly. They seemed very agitated. I left the table and walked to the end of the corridor and peered outside. The Soviet drivers were huddled together in little groups whispering to themselves. American officials rushed from their offices to different parts of the building. There was another crisis in the consul's office. A young Soviet man had refused to leave. He claimed to have a bomb.

Very little was known about Yuri Vlasenko. He was twenty-seven, a merchant seaman, and had come to the embassy looking for help in emigrating. When negotiations failed, Soviet guards were called in and, apparently, told, "It is your responsibility. You must handle it the way you see fit."

First, the Soviet guards tear-gassed the room where the seaman had taken shelter. When that failed, a marksman was called. Two shots were fired. Yuri Vlasenko then pulled the pin and detonated the bomb, killing himself. All we know is that he wanted to leave the Soviet Union and that he is dead.

In the *New York Times,* David K. Shipler wrote that U.S. Ambassador Toon then constituted regulations making it virtually impossible for Soviet citizens to enter the embassy. Before the Vlasenko incident, diplomats from the embassy regularly escorted Soviets past the guards at the front gates. "Now," wrote Shipler, "U.S. diplomats appear unwilling to continue their practice for unknown Russians, partly because of the physical risk and partly because the officer who escorted the man (Vlasenko) into the embassy grounds has received a negative efficiency report that is expected to damage his career."

In June 1979, Vladimir Bukovsky commented about such incidents, including our own case, in a speech in America. It was part of his address to the Coalition for a Democratic Majority and is included in Senator Levin's bill and in the Congressional Record.

> Every day at the gates of the embassy, people are arrested, despite the Consular Convention between the United States and the USSR, which provides "free access" to the U.S. Embassy. The American government is not brave enough to insist on the observance of this agreement. In view of this, I would like to ask the American people, to whom do you send your envoys? To the people of our country or to its executioners?

During our stay in the embassy, there were several incidents at the gates. There were about ten to fifteen "accidents," some with fatal results, over the most intensive period.[33]

One afternoon a Soviet family approached the embassy. Their three children were between five and nine years old. They were stopped by the Soviet militia at the gates. One policeman grabbed the woman, and four policemen dragged the father behind her. The little children ran from the mother to the father, crying and pleading with the militia to let them go. Their parents also cried. It was such a pitiful sight. I never found out their names or where they are now.

On another afternoon, a Soviet lady, quite large in size, tried to enter the embassy. At the same time, an embassy car driven by one of the Soviet drivers was approaching the gate. Noticing the lady trying to rush in, the driver swerved toward her pinning her to the wall and crushing her. The woman gave a loud, sharp scream and collapsed, blood streaming from her wounds. I could hear the militia men talking. "She's dead," one said to the other as they called for other policemen to come and help them carry her lifeless body away. A few minutes later the driver, having parked the car inside the compound and after observing this scene, walked over to the militia men and apologized for causing them more work.[34]

I have reported only a few of the incidents; I can personally verify many others. Should we allow ourselves to become immune to such misfortune and sadness? These situations occur. We must not turn our heads and pretend they will mysteriously stop. Reality must be faced. If our politicians make the rules, they must face the consequences. The issue of emigration is serious. So also is the need to uphold the law so that innocent people are not victimized. People everywhere need to make a determined resolve to end such tyranny and to provide support for the victims. Special responsibility lies on those who undertake negotiations with the Soviet authorities.

When Alexandr Solzhenitsyn addressed union leaders at an AFL-CIO meeting in New York in 1975, he said, "If they bury us alive in the ground, please do not send them shovels. Please do not sent them up-to-date earth-moving equipment."

7

The Siberian Seven

John Pollock called his book *The Siberian Seven*. It was finally published in England in 1979.[35] In the prologue, he described his first meeting with us:

> It was a bitterly cold day and we were all frozen. Our meeting was held outside in the courtyard and I spoke to them through an interpreter.
>
> I was impressed by their genuineness, gentleness, courage and sterling Christian faith, and also by a half-hidden sense of humor, despite their troubles. I was touched to learn afterward that they worried a little lest their terrible situation might have made them seem, to me, gloomy and humorless. I was also sorry to hear that they came down with colds after the open-air meeting because they didn't have warm clothes at that point.

I was face to face with people that I had written about over fifteen years ago. I knew now that they had a remarkable story.

The first time that I was handed a copy of the book was a special moment in my life. I believed that it had the potential to unite the support that had been accumulating for us and break the stalemate that had developed in our case. The book was a public, visible reminder of our existence. It was able to speak for us while we were forbidden to meet with people. It could enter doors that we were unable to approach.

The Siberian Seven was based on our writings. In the text John explained:

> Eventually they wrote many hundreds of pages, amounting to more than 250,000 words (in English translation). This is the fullest single account in manuscript of such matters ever to be received in the West.
>
> Their testimony is supported all the way through by official documents they brought with them. The scraps of evidence that have filtered from all over the Soviet Union for years past show a remarkable similarity as evidence of repression and discrimination against believers. Yet never before has it been possible to follow in close detail the fortune of one group, among the thousands who have experienced the full force of the state's determination to make atheism supreme.
>
> The Vashchenkos' and Chmykhalovs' sufferings reveal the truth in its starkness as no general assessment, no patchwork of evidence, may hope to do. "The Siberian Seven" therefore have a significance far beyond the thrill and pain of their own adventures.

They wrote with a full realization of the risk to themselves if their hope of emigration is denied. They wrote for the sake of all believers and wherever the Seven's future lies, in the West or still in the Soviet Union, their story demands attention.

The Siberian Seven featured the Vashchenko family's story extensively. Perhaps a second book would explain more about our family. Perhaps a second book would not be needed.

Despite the Soviet Union's sensitivity to public opinion, the publication of the book did little to change their mind about our request for exit visas. It did, however, inform more Christians around the world that our case was still unsolved. With the publication of the book came media coverage of our case. The press attention did more to embarrass the Americans than the Soviets. If somehow, it was suggested, the tables could be turned, the Soviet government would be quick to consider ways of resolving our case. The spotlight was turned on the Americans. It was their "problem."

I noticed from some of the news clippings that we were shown by friends that we received as much coverage in Europe as we did in America. Even John Pollock's book was not published in America for some time. I found it very strange that many Americans still did not know about us, despite the hard work of many people and organizations. We were a well-kept secret. So I was naturally surprised—and pleased—when I was shown an article and the text of a radio broadcast by a prominent American figure who spoke directly about us:

> It is difficult for me to say this, but it is true that most Americans are unaware that last year, 1979, seven Pente-

costal Christians were confined in a twelve by twenty-foot room in the U.S. Embassy in Moscow. They were taken there because they wanted to leave Russia—that country had become too oppressive. Until recently they weren't allowed embassy food, but a couple of embassy employees would go out and stand in the lines for them and buy food for them.

The Ambassador at the time tried to persuade them into going out and turning themselves over to the Russian secret police. But this of course would have meant their death. Yet he tried just the same—apparently they had become an embarrassment to him.

Can you imagine such a thing? The behavior of someone selected to represent a country established by Almighty God who was embarrassed because seven Christians were fleeing from spiritual strangulation.

I want to see a State Department that will encourage such people, that will say to them, "America is still the land of freedom under God," This is a fundamental right as far as I am concerned, the worship of the Creator without whom we wouldn't be as blessed as we are in this nation.

I read the transcript quickly and reread it again. It had the tone of the broadcasts that we had heard from Voice of America, broadcasts that had originally encouraged us to seek help from the embassy. Perhaps at last we had found one who would defend us and fight for our right to leave the Soviet Union.

The text of the radio broadcasts concluded with a pertinent question: "Detente is supposed to be a two-way street. Our wheat and technology can get into Russia—why can't the Vashchenko and Chmykhalov families get out?"

I asked our friend who had brought the transcript about the author of these words. I was told, "His name is Ronald Reagan. He used to be a movie actor in Hollywood. He is now the Republican candidate for the presidency of the United States. He could well be our next president."

At the time I was unfamiliar with election campaigning. The Soviet Union has one party, one candidate, and one seat. The campaigns are necessarily somewhat differently organized. In America, President Jimmy Carter was known as a "born again" Christian and an outspoken advocate of human rights. For the first time, I followed the American elections very closely. If Reagan became president, I reasoned, that would give him the power to institute proceedings to resolve our case or at least to begin serious discussions with the Soviets about us.

The first change we noticed was a new photograph being hung in the consul's waiting room where we usually placed our telephone calls to Chernogorsk. I don't know how much President Reagan helped us at first. Perhaps if some extra power had been exerted in those early days of his presidency, our case would have been resolved sooner. But one recent development in our case guaranteed that President Reagan would not be allowed to forget us: the introduction of Bill S.2890 into the U.S. Senate.[36]

8

US Senate Bill

On June 27, 1980, we marked our second year in the embassy with prayer and fasting. Events in Washington on that same day stirred our hearts to hope that this would be our last "unhappy anniversary." Senator Carl Levin introduced Bill S.2890 into the U.S. Senate that would give all seven of us permanent residence in the embassy. Several resolutions mentioning us had been introduced in Congress, but S.2890 took the support one step further.

During Easter 1979, we had received our first visit from American members of Congress, Jack Edwards and Richard Shelby. Later other members of Congress were allowed to meet us. In August 1979, Carl Levin, accompanied by Senator David Boren, spent some time talking with us. Both senators assured us of their support. Before he left us, Mr. Levin said, "I will do everything I can to help you. I will not forget you." He was one man who was true to his word. When he returned home, he stayed in touch with our case and instigated several initiatives. In May 1980, Senator Levin (and fifty other senators) signed a joint letter of appeal to President Brezhnev, requesting that our visas be granted.[37]

One month later, Bill S.2890 was introduced into Congress. It was significant in four specific areas.

First, it provided a focal point for the support that was accumulating for us: The more support for the bill, the greater the pressure on President Reagan to begin serious discussions with the Soviets about us. The more media attention and coverage that we received, the greater the awareness among the general public, who were encouraged to write to their senators requesting support for S.2890 (the bill was reintroduced as S.312 in the new session)

Second, the bill cleared up many of the misunderstandings that had arisen surrounding our case. It amplified the complexities and sought, for the first time, to explain the facts. It clarified our rights regarding emigration and the reasons why we had become "guests" of the embassy.

Third, the legislation explained the tensions that had arisen between the embassy staff and us. The legislation stated, "The alienation they have experienced in the embassy has made them outcasts in the very place they seek refuge."

Fourth, the bill dealt with the issue that most concerned the American diplomats. They feared that if we emigrated directly from the embassy basement, a precedent would be set. This was explained in a letter I had written and which was now included in Senator Frank Church's Senate Report.

On July 24 we met with four Dutch correspondents; one, who spoke Russian, was our interpreter. The consulate forbade the correspondents to take any pictures. We were never left alone with the correspondents, and all written documents that we wanted to show them had to be read in advance by an officer from the consular section. When the correspondents asked the officer whether the embassy had been doing something on our behalf and whether it would let us emigrate directly from the embassy, the officer replied, "If we let them leave directly from the embassy, the whole of Siberia will invade the embassy."

That proves to us that the embassy neither wishes, nor wants, nor works to permit us to emigrate from the USSR. The embassy wants to achieve its goal which is to escort us politely and diplomatically from the embassy (to make us leave). And what then? Evidently the answer does not seem to worry the embassy. All they want is to make us leave, politely, and send us back to Chernogorsk to file our application there.[38]

Bill S.2890 dealt squarely with the problem that was causing concern. It stated, "This legislation is tightly controlled so that it cannot become a broad precedent for other possible asylum-refugee seekers." The "precedent issue" was clearly important to the U.S. government's policy making regarding our situation.

The dilemma for us was equally real. We had come to the embassy to plead for help from people all over the free world, and to the American embassy in particular because they said that they would help people like us. Our situation was complex; our case deadlocked. But our lives were in peril and the evidence was overwhelming. This is the internationally recognized justification for seeking and obtaining asylum.[39] We had broken no law by trying to enter the embassy. America and the Soviet Union had signed a Consular Convention. This guaranteed "free access" to the gates of the Consul Section. In fact, the Soviets were breaking their own law by preventing us from entering the embassy. In the great halls of our nation, politicians sign pledges and make laws. In reality when the promises they have made are inconvenient, they blink.

We did not burst into the embassy demanding permission to emigrate, an image that has circulated widely in the West. If John Vashchenko had not been beaten and abducted, we would not have remained inside the embassy building. If this key point and our legal rights, according to the Helsinki Final Act and the Consular Convention, had been clarified, much confusion would have been avoided and the process for securing exit visas would have begun without fear of establishing a precedent or allowing unwarranted embassy sit-ins. But for some reason, the U.S. government chose not to publicize the essential facts about the case, even though they were precisely the facts that could have alleviated any real concern over a new precedent.

Senator Levin's introduction of this bill also challenged the embassy policy that suggested our case would be solved if we left the building and returned home. Of course, the problem for the American Embassy would be solved. But would our emigration case be resolved? Instead of pressuring the Soviet government to honor international law and permit us to emigrate, the Americans actually pressured us to leave the embassy. One of the particularly difficult moments came when one of the embassy staff challenged us to leave, saying, "Who's going to be the first to leave and go back to Chernogorsk?" This incident was reported by Dan Fischer in the *L.A. Times* and quoted in the Congressional Record of the bill.

Publicly the American Embassy asserted that everything possible was being done to help us. Senator Levin's bill showed how U.S. policy was actually being carried out and that three levels of contact that could have brought us some encouragement and aided our case were denied us: visitors, the mail, and publicity.

Our contact with visitors during the first year was carefully screened. Even embassy personnel were discouraged from talking to us, and we were not permitted to attend church services. Some overseas visitors were permitted a meeting with us, but many others were denied. In an article in the *Birmingham News,* Jane Drake, one of our supporters in America, explained the difficulties. The entire text of this article is also included in the Congressional Record.

> The State Department wanted to keep this thing quiet. They made it very difficult initially for the news media to interview these people. And even Congressman Richard C. Shelby (D-Ala) who went over there this Easter week had trouble seeing them. Mr. Shelby even had a letter from our governor requesting the Congressman be given permission to see these people on behalf of the people of Alabama.
>
> Six senators had already gone to Moscow last January but were not able to see the Vashchenkos. We have a letter from Senator Baker of Tennessee saying he was "reluctantly persuaded" by Malcolm Toon (the Ambassador) not to see the Vashchenkos."[40]

Mrs. Drake wrote about the difficulties she encountered in her efforts to help us.

I remember the first phone call I made to the Moscow Embassy. I talked to a marine embassy guard. I said, "I can't believe that you don't know about those people," and he kept saying, "I have no one by that name on the register." I said, "Of course they're not on the register. They don't work in the embassy, they're in the basement room." He never lost his cool, he stayed totally calm.

We later realized that this man had been instructed to say just what he said. He actually never lied to me. He just continued to go back to that same statement: "They are not on the register."

On December 19, 1979, four prominent British Baptist leaders led by Dr. David Russell were denied permission to visit us. Later the embassy claimed that a junior official had given the order. The next day, however, Mr. Michael Rowe of Keston College was also forbidden a visit. The consul staff told him, "We can't let you visit them after we've refused Dr. Russell." Six days later an embassy employee asked if he could visit us. This request was refused. It was Christmas Day.

The embassy refused to give us any mail that arrived through the diplomatic pouch or that had been sent to us addressed to President Carter at the White House. The embassy's official position was that it would deliver any letters or cards that arrived through the international mail—mail the KGB allowed through. At Christmas 1979, Jane Drake learned that only ten cards trickled through from the several thousand that had been mailed. There is clear documentation that over the years several thousand letters, cards, and parcels had been mailed to us from people all over the world. Very few ever arrived. Despite strong representation from groups in the West, no protest was ever made about the Soviet's interference with the international mail.

Article 56 of the Soviet Constitution guarantees all citizens secrecy of mail. It states:

> The private life of citizens and the secrecy of correspondence, telephone conversations, and telegraph messages are protected by law.

Belgian lawyer, Vincent Van Den Bosch, argued that the embassy should at least show us the mail that had arrived through the diplomatic bag or through other channels. He claimed that the letters may belong to the embassy, but that the contents belonged to us.

The embassy would not allow us to receive mail through the diplomatic bag because it contravened some technicality and so was illegal. But Senator Levin stated, "It astounds me to learn that Soviet citizens who are embassy employees have been able to use a portion of their wages to purchase American goods through American mail order facilities and use the diplomatic pouch to do so. However the Pentecostalists have been told that they cannot use the pouch at any time."

The embassy never called a press conference to clarify some of the misunderstandings that had arisen concerning our case. Publicity, one of the single factors that could assist us, was consistently restricted.[41] Ambassador Toon had forbidden all press photographs to be taken in the basement. Until our first anniversary in June 1979, no television interviews were permitted. When this rule was lifted, interviews were only allowed in the embassy compound, regardless of weather conditions.

In December 1980, Jane Drake was granted special permission: a telephone call to us at Christmas. This was at the intervention of Senator Levin. The CBS news program "Sixty Minutes" had planned to feature our case and wished to record the telephone call. This request was refused.

Michael Hart, a producer with ATV in England, had planned a feature television program for July 15, Lilya Vashchenko's twenty-fourth birthday. Days before the program was recorded, Hart was informed that the State Department had vetoed the call that was to be filmed for the show. A spokesman said, "There is an embargo on recording and broadcasting telephone calls with the seven."

The objective of Senator Levin's bill was to seek permanent residence for us in the embassy. Senator Levin stated, "Our legislation will issue these seven courageous people American visas and would allow them to be admitted to the United States for permanent residence." I understood that the bill would not have guaranteed our emigration, but it would have made our stay in the embassy more secure. It would have transformed grace to sanctuary.

For me, the most encouraging factor of the bill was that for the first time, someone was taking our case seriously. This was the first earnest attempt made to resolve our problem.

9

Dead-End Street

In July, one month after the introduction of S.2890 to the U.S. Senate, the ambassador circulated a memo to the section chiefs at the embassy. It was a policy statement that came to be included in the Congressional Record of Senator Frank Church's Report.[42] The memo clarified the situation concerning visits to our basement. A written request to the consul was required. "My general approach is not to expand the list (of those who could visit us) so in many cases it may be necessary for interested families to wait until someone drops from the list." It also emphasized that no photos or tape recordings could be made "for publicity purposes."

In October 1980, Moscow played host to an international event. The spectacle of the Olympic Games was heralded as a symbol of world unity, of the setting aside of political differences. But staring through the barred window at

Muscovites strolling outside, I wondered how real such images could be.

The Soviets cleaned up the city for the thousands of visitors that were expected. Along with the rubbish and dirt, all those considered a potential risk were arrested or forced to move out of Moscow. This included many Christians. How can we stand silently on the sidelines, watching the parade go by? Can such events really be separated from issues of freedom and human rights and justice?

The Olympics marked yet another opportunity for the Soviets to resolve our case, to give the West a sign of their serious intentions concerning the issue of human rights. But it was not to be.

Perhaps Senator Levin realized that the bill would not pass easily through the Senate (in fact, when it came to open hearings, it was opposed by the State Department). To alleviate our immediate situation, he took one further step. On September 30, 1980, Senator Levin instigated a letter of appeal, signed by forty-one senators and addressed to Edmund Muskie, secretary of state. The letter crystallized the major issues of tension between the embassy and us and appealed for the authorities to relax the conditions that had been imposed on us.

In December 1980, another attempt was made to persuade us to leave the embassy. This "suggestion" came with the visit of Senator Charles Percy. Percy had cosigned a letter from fifty senators addressed to President Brezhnev in support of our case, but did not cosign Senator Levin's bill. He asked us to sign a letter in which we promised to leave the basement and return home to Chernogorsk. Then Senator Percy promised he would intercede on our behalf with the Kremlin. We considered his offer and politely refused. One journalist remarked that Senator Percy may have been an expert on Soviet affairs, but that we had lived with Soviet reality.

Kevin Lynch published an article in the April 3, 1981 issue of the *National Review,* commenting on Senator Percy's visit and the embassy's "background paper" prepared for his visit.[43] The paper, Lynch pointed out, stated that we were extremely suspicious about the U.S. government's motives toward us because of the precedent issue. Lynch writes, "Perhaps the families can be forgiven their suspicion; a member of the embassy's Consular Section had told a Western correspondent, in the presence of the seven, 'If we let them leave directly from the embassy, all Siberia would descend on us.' "

The background paper reiterated the embassy's position (which also happened to be the Soviet one) that we could only pursue our emigration by returning home to Siberia but did not state why we refused to return home.

I do not want to turn this into an inquest on the American Embassy or the U.S. government. I am deeply grateful that they granted me refuge in the embassy. It probably saved my life. I am also thankful to many people at the embassy who were sympathetic to us and tried to help us and encourage us in many different ways.

Perhaps from all this we can learn that some situations have to be faced and need to be resolved while they are still small and manageable. Those who sit in power should not be insensitive to the needs of the poor and the unjustly oppressed. Also, the law must be honored and not be allowed to become a mockery such as the pattern set by the Soviet Union where the phenomenon of the law is relevant to two groups: those who enforce it, and those who are above it.

Why did we refuse to leave the embassy? What would have happened if we had listened to the American Embassy's advice and returned to Siberia during this time? When we talked to our families in Chernogorsk on the telephone, we learned that lectures about us were already under way in the factories and shops. They warned the people of Chernogorsk, "Get ready, the enemies of our nation and traitors of our Fatherland will soon be returning." So the people in our hometown were being incited against our family. Local authorities openly threatened to imprison members of our family.

In a letter addressed to friends in the West, and now included in the U.S. Senate Report, I explained:

> We are sure that as soon as we leave the embassy we'll be in the hands of the KGB and taken for interrogation. As (Galina Stepanovna) Andriushchenko in Chernogorsk said, "As soon as we leave the embassy we shall be arrested on the spot, and so will everybody in our family. This is what will happen."[44]

On February 19, 1980, I spoke with Nadezhda, and my aunt, who were in the local post office in Chernogorsk. My aunt told me about an article that had been written about us in *Chernogorsk Rabochi* (the *Chernogorsk Worker*), our local paper, under the heading "At a Dead End." The article alleged that our family in Chernogorsk had renounced my mother and me. It also stated that a member of the U.S. Embassy in Moscow had told an American correspondent that we are fanatics. The correspondent had allegedly then asked some American believers how they felt about accepting us. The American believers had replied, "They are not our headache. Do with them what you want." The correspondent had supposedly published this story in the newspaper, and the Soviet journalist claimed that he was quoting from this paper for his own article in *Chernogorsk Rabochi.*

The Soviet newspaper article concluded, "The two families went to the embassy, but found themselves in a dead-end street. American believers do not want to accept them, and they do not want to leave the embassy. They are afraid of punishment for what they have done."

The words seemed to ring in my ears: Dead-End Street . . . Dead-End Street . . . *Trapped in a Dead-End Street.*

10

Papa Threatened in Chernogorsk

It was September 1981. The room was stuffy. I felt I had to get out and go for a walk. Anywhere. It didn't matter. I walked to the window and looked outside. It was a warm day, and the people walking on the pavement outside were wearing light summer clothes. I felt caged.

"What's on television?" Lyuba asked, breaking the silence in the room. She was referring to the window. She walked over to the corner of the room and picked up a guitar that had been sent through a friend visiting Moscow. Sitting on the edge of the bed opposite my mother, she began to pluck the strings of the guitar, picking out a melody.

Lyuba was an extremely accomplished girl. She was experienced in dress-making and had mastered English; she had a sharp mind and usually dealt with journalists' questions and with the American diplomats. She called

Lidiya and Lilya over to her and together the three began to sing. Peter and Augustina were by the sink preparing food, but they listened intently to their daughters' voices as they sang. My mother, who had spent the entire morning knitting, also paused. It was an old gospel song that we had often sung at church services, and it brought back memories of home.

I thought about the news that we had received that morning. Papa had called on the telephone. I talked first and then left the consul's office so that Mama could have some privacy when she spoke to him. Papa's voice had been serious. He usually had some joke or funny story to cheer us up. This time, his words had a dark and sinister tone.

"They've threatened to arrest me once again," he said halfway through our conversation. "I didn't want to worry you and your mother, but I thought you ought to know."

"What happened?" I asked him. The telephone line was particularly bad on this occasion, and we were both shouting into the receiver. We generally assumed that the KGB was listening in on our conversations and were never surprised when some calls were abruptly terminated midsentence.

Papa explained that Lt. Dmitrev, a divisional police inspector in Chernogorsk, and three *druzhiniki* (voluntary militia assistants) called at our home on September 8, 1981, at eight in the evening and took him to the police station. There they tried to pressure him into signing a document stating that he confessed to living without a passport, thus violating the passport procedure. When my father refused to sign the statement, Dmitrev telephoned his superiors. After some discussion, the police inspector told my father that he could return home but warned, "Tomorrow we will begin court proceedings against you to put you on trial."

I didn't know what to say. I knew that the police had threatened Papa several times—this was the very reason why we had decided to travel to Moscow to ask for help from the American Embassy in 1978.

"Pray for me, Timothy," Papa said, "and if you are able, ask our friends to pray for us. Tell them what is happening here." Papa sounded scared, and I felt frustrated and helpless. I prayed silently. I also prayed for Mama. I worried about her. Sometimes she would get very depressed. She would stare for hours out of the window, locked away with her secret thoughts. Once I saw her standing outside the room sobbing. "I wonder if I'll ever live long enough to see my grandchildren," she whispered—Vladimir and Katharina now had two children, Roman and Yelena. Already the psychological strain was beginning to show. If Papa were arrested, it would shatter the slender thread between hope and despair.

I began to pace nervously around the room. But in the confined space, I quickly realized that I was disturbing the others. I picked up one of the new books by Alexandr Solzhenitsyn that one of our visitors had given us. Solzhenitsyn is considered a folk hero by the people, but a traitor by the Soviet authorities. His books are popular and circulate underground through samizdat (self-publishing), although it's a criminal offense to be caught with such subversive literature.

In fifteen minutes I had read only two pages—I just couldn't concentrate. I found myself turning the page and not knowing what I had just read. I replaced the book on my shelf with the few other books that I had managed to collect and started to think again about Papa's words. What was it that he had said? "Ask people to pray for me."

Immediately, I knew what I must do. I grabbed my notebook and walked toward the door. Settling myself on a box, I began to compose a letter. I knew it was necessary to be as factual as possible, but I had difficulty writing in English. I had only recently become a little more proficient in English. I had been given a picture book as my first lesson in learning the language. It had been prepared for children and really was very basic: A is for Apple, B is for Ball, and so forth. At first I had found the English language quite simple and could follow some of the conversations in the embassy. But gradually it became more difficult. The grammar and tenses were difficult to use, and I found it hard to remember words. I spent the morning and afternoon of most days trying to learn verbs, pronouns, adjectives and memorize phrases.

It took me some time to complete the letter because I had to consult the Russian-English dictionary frequently to check spellings. I made a rough draft of the letter, checked it over for mistakes, and then recopied it. I suspected that, despite my efforts, my grammar needed correction. Just as I was puzzling over how to end the letter, I heard footsteps along the corridor. We had a visitor.

In 1981, the restrictions placed on us by the embassy had been relaxed, perhaps by Senator Levin's initiatives and the increase in media attention. We were permitted more visitors, and eventually they were allowed to call on us in the basement. Permission had to be obtained through the consul's office, but it was usually granted. Press correspondents in Moscow found it easier to interview us. We were also given odd jobs around the embassy and freer movement in the building and the compound; we were even permitted to receive overseas telephone calls from our supporters in the West—the first telephone call was from Jane Drake in Alabama.

After our appeal to Pope John Paul II, we were permitted to attend church services on Sunday. This was quite a breakthrough and gave us a way to make contact with staff members and visitors, some of whom were quite sympathetic toward us. It became an important way for us to communicate with people. Even our presence at the service served as a reminder that our case was still unresolved. But we always had to be careful in our approach because people were generally not encouraged to help us.

Our visitor on the day of my father's telephone call had read an article about us in a Christian magazine earlier that year. Since then he had followed our case. He was visiting Moscow and Leningrad, on holiday with a tour group, and decided to visit us. He spent some time talking with Lyuba, as she knew English better than any of us. After a while he walked over to me and asked what I was writing. I explained and asked if he could help me to complete my letter.

"Sure," he replied and read through the few paragraphs I had written, making comments and notes as he did so. In a few minutes the new letter was completed. I thanked him, but he brushed aside my thanks. "It's nothing. It's my pleasure."

"How will you mail it from here?" he asked. "Will the embassy mail it for you?"

"No," I replied, "it's a problem to mail letters to our friends."

He then explained that he would be leaving Moscow in two days, but if I wished, he would call in to see us before leaving to collect my letter. When he reached the West, he would mail it.

"Thank you, Lord," I whispered.

That night I stayed up trying to complete the letter and making as many copies as I could. I addressed letters to a few friends in America and Europe and added a short note. "Please publish this news and circulate it to anyone you can. Ask people to pray and work for my father." I didn't know if my letter would be published in a newspaper, end up in an editor's filing tray, or worse still, in an "out" tray on someone's desk.

While some groups, organizations, and churches seemed reluctant to become involved with our case, Jane Drake, a young housewife in Alabama, was still fired with energy. She had now assumed responsibility for an organization entitled SAVE (Society for Americans for Vashchenko's Emigration). The organization had an impressive title but much of the workload fell on Jane's shoulder. She worked tirelessly, and at times single-handedly, to publicize the case of both our families in the early days before the media attention began to focus on us.

Senator Levin's bill had been proposed by Olga and Blahoshav Hruby, who published a journal in New York entitled *Religion in Communist Dominated Lands*. Many of our families' letters were published in this journal for the first time. Also in Zurich, Marianna Ridge worked persistently for us, even after working hours at Christian Solidarity International, where she was employed. And in 1981, the launch of the London-based Campaign to Free the Siberian Seven was created. These were not the only people active on our behalf. It would, however, take another book to report fairly on all those who played a part.

"Lord," I prayed that night as I folded each letter and addressed each envelope, "please direct these letters to those who will help our family."

"When our darling daughter, Rebekah, was born on August 18, 1984, I felt that it was for such a moment our family had struggled. Twenty years before it seemed like a dream."
Timothy and Tatyana Chmykhalov, with Rebekah

"Maria met and fell in love with a short, wiry coal miner, four years her junior, named Peter Sergeevich Chmykhalov." Timothy's parents, a photograph made about 1969 when his father was in exile

Peter Chmykhalov standing in front of Timothy's home in Chernogorsk, a city in southeast Siberia near the Mongolian border

"They built a house at Twentieth Khakassia Year Street, in the settlement at Mine Nine where Mama worked. This settlement developed into a suburb of Chernogorsk, and was called Chernogorsk-1."

"Peter and Maria named their first child Nadezhda; she was to be the only girl in a family of five." Four of the five Chmykhalov children with Maria; from the left are Alexander, Maria, and Timothy, with Nadezhda and Anatoly standing in the back.

"On the wall facing us was a large, framed, color photograph of the President of the United States: the smiling face of Jimmy Carter peered down on us." One month after the seven came to the embassy, this photograph was released to the West. (July, 1978)

"In August 1979, Carl Levin, accompanied by Senator David Boren, spent some time talking with us. Before he left us, Mr. Levin said, 'I will do everything I can to help you. I will not forget you.' In May 1980, Senator Levin (and fifty other senators) signed a joint letter of appeal to President Brezhnev, requesting that our visas be granted." Timothy, Senator Levin, Alexander

The first "Free the Siberian Seven" campaign was held in a London church, Kensington Temple. A demonstration followed, in front of the Russian Embassy. (Photography by Mick Rock, Cephas Picture Library. Used by permission.)

Peter Meadows, English publisher of popular *Buzz* magazine, speaks at the campaign known as Human Wrongs Day. His magazine ran stories about what had happened both in the embassy and in Siberia to the Chmykhalov and the Vashchenko families. (Photography by Mick Rock, Cephas Picture Library. Used by permission.)

Soviet dissident Alexander Ginzburg speaks at the 1982 Human Wrongs Day campaign in London. (Photography by Mick Rock, Cephas Picture Library. Used by permission.)

Danny Smith, coauthor of *The Last Christian*, holds up a copy of Moscow's newspaper, *Pravda*, during the Human Wrongs Day rally. The Siberian Seven were still in the embassy basement. (Photography by Mick Rock, Cephas Picture Library. Used by permission.)

Dr. George Hobbs, one of the medical doctors who visited the Siberian Seven in the American Embassy, addresses a March 6, 1982, rally in Trafalgar Square. The banner on the heart-shaped bag of balloons in the background read, "Have a Heart Mr. Brezhnev, Free the Siberian Seven." (Photography by Mick Rock, Cephas Picture Library. Used by permission.)

"We were not famous dissidents, celebrated scientists, human rights activists, intellectuals, writers or politicians. We were two ordinary Christian families." The Siberian Seven: from left to right, Timothy Chmykhalov and Lidiya, Lilya, and Lyuba Vashchenko (seated); Maria Chmykhalov and Augustina and Peter Vashchenko (standing)

"The room had a tiny, barred window overlooking Chaikovskovo Street where the Soviet militia patrolled. It was the only view of the world outside."

"Mr. George Bush, Vice President of the United States, smiled and shook my hand. 'You're almost as tall as I am,' he said jokingly. Standing beside him was Mr. George Schultz, Secretary of State."

THE WHITE HOUSE
WASHINGTON

April 5, 1983

Dear Friends:

I want you to know that I join with you in rejoicing at Lidia's recent departure from the Soviet Union. We are hopeful that all of you will soon be able to join her in a land where you may freely express and practice your deeply-held religious beliefs.

Dr. Olin Robison, the bearer of this letter, is one whom you know and respect as a wise and honorable man who has the deepest regard for your welfare. Let me tell you that he also has my full confidence and support. I commend his advice to you and urge you to accept it.

This letter also provides me the opportunity to thank you for the lovely embroidered picture that you sent to Nancy and me as a Christmas gift. We very much appreciated your thoughtfulness.

In conclusion, I wish to reiterate my full support for your desire to emigrate and to serve God as you choose. I pray that these desires may soon be realized for all of you. Godspeed!

Sincerely,

Ronald Reagan

The Chmykhalov Family
American Embassy
Moscow

Lidiya left the embassy in January of 1982 due to complications from a hunger strike. This letter from President Reagan acknowledged Lidiya's departure from the Soviet Union a year later, an event that foreshadowed the future departure of all seven dissidents. Dr. Olin Robison carried news from his meeting with Soviet Ambassador Anatoliy Dobrynin.

Danny Smith, his wife Joan, and Timothy wait outside 10 Downing Street to greet Prime Minister Margaret Thatcher and thank her for her involvement in the release of the Seven, which included an offer for them to come and live in England. (Photography by Mick Rock, Cephas Picture Library. Used by permission.)

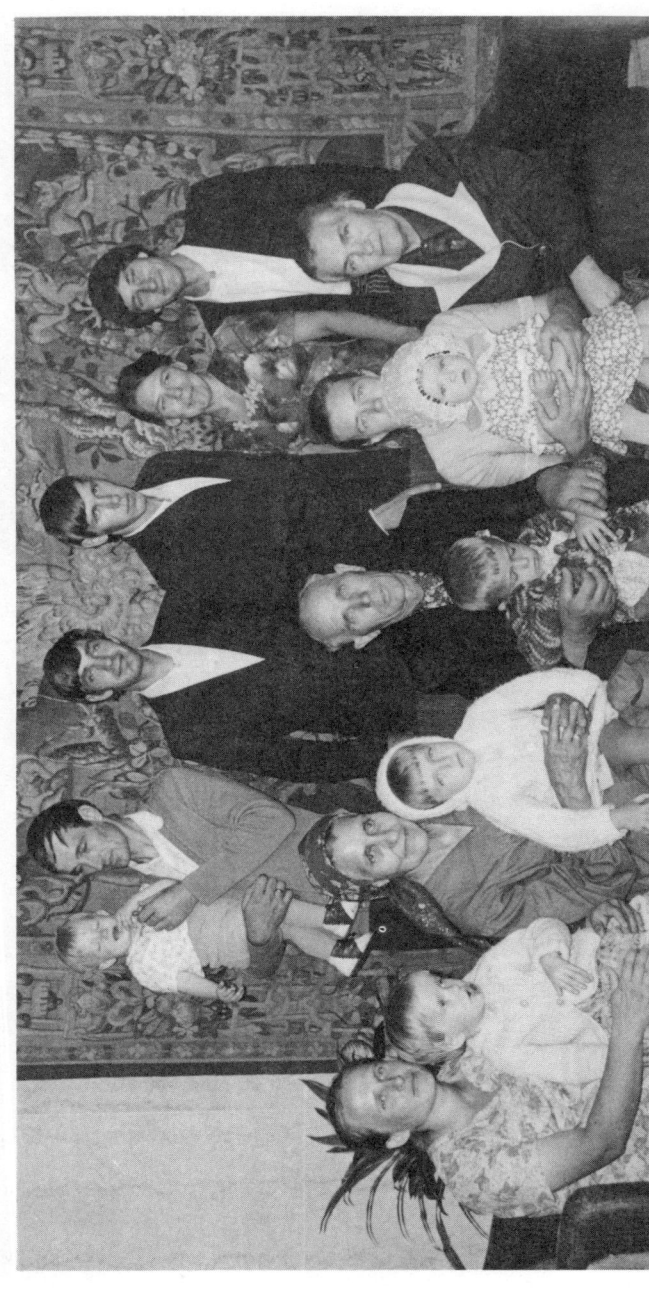

Freedom for the Siberian Seven meant freedom for the Chmykhalov family; they were photographed at the Vienna airport after their release from the Soviet Union. Those in the back row include (from the left) brothers Vladimir, Anatoly, Timothy (and wife Tatyana), and Alexander. Seated in the front row are Vladimir's wife Katrina, parents Maria and Peter, sister Nadezhda, and Aunt Anna.

After leaving Europe, Timothy arrived in Dallas, Texas, and was welcomed at Christ for the Nations Institute by its president, Freida Lindsey. (August 12, 1983)

The family of Timothy's wife, Tatyana, a photograph made in 1983 in Chernogorsk; sister Galina and mother Alexandra (seated), and sister Nadezhda

"What has surprised you the most since you arrived in the West?" The girl who asked the question was a young college student sitting in the front row of the church where I had been invited to speak.

11

Hunger Strike

Lidiya looked pale and weak. She sat quietly on one corner of the bed. The light from the basement window illuminated the room with the last dying rays of the sun. Her Bible lay open in her lap, and she squinted occasionally as she read silently to herself. Augustina sat beside her, talking to Peter, who stood in the center of the room.

For several days now, both mother and daughter had been taking no nourishment other than tea and light juices. On Christmas day 1981, Augustina began the fast and then a few days later, Lidiya joined her. At first this went unnoticed, but after a few days, it became international news. Almost daily, different foreign correspondents visited the basement to talk to the two women.

I heard both Augustina and Lidiya say to the newspeople that they would not stop the hunger strike. Lidiya told Steven Hurst, "I hold this hunger strike against both governments to make them pay attention and solve the question of our emigration." This was because the American Embassy officials were insisting that there was nothing more that they could do and that it was up to the Soviet authorities to grant exit visas. But the Soviet government was silent.

After two weeks had passed, the seriousness of the situation was apparent to all. Friends and supporters in the West became concerned for the health of both women. Some encouraged them to end the hunger strike; several called to speak to them on the telephone. At one point, former president Jimmy Carter placed a telephone call to the embassy and spoke to the Vashchenko family requesting their ending the hunger strike. Still, nothing could change their minds.

Augustina told one reporter, "I don't know how many days I can survive. If the children in Chernogorsk are sent abroad and we hear about it, then our hunger strike will stop."

I stood in the corridor outside the basement room. I didn't know what to think. How would this end? I stepped aside to allow two of the correspondents to pass on their way out of the room. One of the reporters held a camera in his hand. They paused for a moment to talk to me. "Do you want to give up and go home?" one asked. "Have you lost hope?"

It didn't take me a minute to reply. "No, No," I said quickly. Not for one moment did I ever think of leaving. I knew the consequences if we left the embassy. I didn't know why I had been chosen to spend these last two and a half years in the basement, but I felt God would not abandon us.

I said, "If history was to repeat itself. I would do the same thing all over again. I have no regrets."

On January 22, 1982, this report from Nigel Wade in Moscow appeared in London's *Daily Telegraph:*

> The hunger strikers, who have been on a diet of tea and fruit juice to dramatize their demand for exit visas, sat knitting yesterday. They felt weak but were still "okay."
>
> The Pentecostalists want the American and Russian government to break a diplomatic deadlock and find a solution to their plight. American officials say they are doing everything to help, but the Pentecostalists are not convinced.
>
> "We have given people enough time to do something," said Lidiya Vashchenko yesterday. They realize they may have to be taken to the hospital but will never go voluntarily.
>
> She added that like anyone "we feel afraid." Her mother said it seemed that a sacrifice was needed.

How long could it last? It was painful to watch both Augustina and Lidiya suffering in this way. A spokesman from the embassy told one reporter: "They are getting close to what we would term a life-threatening situation. Once we determine that they are in that situation, then we would have to take some action."

On January 30, the embassy made that decision. Lidiya was to leave us. She had become severely weakened, and the embassy had decided to put her in the hospital.

I said good-by to Lidiya, feeling both anxious and sad. I was worried for her. I didn't know what would happen to her once she left the safety of the embassy. I knew she was taking a tremendous risk. I felt sad because, despite any difficulties and tensions that existed between our families as a result of our close confinement, we were brothers and sisters in Christ.

Amidst international publicity, Lidiya was driven to Botkin Hospital with Kurt Strubble, the vice-consul and Dr. Shadler, the American doctor at the embassy. Botkin Hospital was generally used by foreign nationals who fall ill in Moscow. Steven Hurst filed this report:

> The 31-year-old woman looked pale and drawn. Lidiya has had no solid foods since the Christmas holidays and only unsweetened tea since last Sunday. Embassy officials said she had lost one tenth of her body weight and was down to about 90 pounds.
>
> Before leaving the embassy, Lidiya thanked the embassy and "all the people of the West who have helped." Then she was driven in a black van to Moscow's Botkin Hospital. On arrival, a hospital aide in a bloodstained white laboratory coat opened the front door, admitting Lidiya, a consular officer, and the American Embassy doctor.
>
> Half a dozen American reporters tried to go into the hospital admitting room with them but were shoved back at the front door by a large Soviet man dressed in white.[45]

A deep melancholy fell over the room once Lidiya had left. There are moments when no words of consolation can convey one's feelings. The Vashchenkos drew strength and comfort from God alone.

The next few days passed quietly. The hospital provided Lidiya with good nourishment and care. The international media continued to follow the case as people in the West extended their prayers and pressure.

Two weeks later in an unprecedented twist, the Soviet authorities allowed Lidiya to return to the embassy to say a brief farewell before returning home. She was accompanied by Vera and Alexander who had traveled down from Chernogorsk to take their elder sister home.

The Associated Press report stated:

Moscow Feb 11.—Miss Lidiya Vashchenko, the Siberian Pentecostalist, was reunited with her family yesterday in the United States Embassy, after treatment in a Moscow hospital for the effects of a month-long hunger strike.

A black embassy van carrying Miss Vashchenko and a brother and sister drove past Soviet police guards into the compound where they were met by their parents and two sisters. They embraced and wept in the courtyard before walking to the basement room where Lidiya, two sisters, and her parents have lived since June 1978, while seeking Soviet exit visas.

Lidiya, who is 30, was released shortly after noon from Botkin hospital were she had been under treatment for almost two weeks. She was taken there by American officials who feared her life was in danger. She and her mother started the hunger strike during the Christmas holidays to protest against what they described as lack of United States pressure on the Soviet government on their behalf.

A United States Embassy official said: "The embassy has reason to be pleased with Soviet treatment of Lidiya from the time she was admitted to the hospital until today." The official said that the Soviet government had been informed of their wish to visit their parents in the embassy but that there had been no statement from the Russians that they would be permitted to enter. "We did not know they would be let in until they drove through the gate" the official said.

Vera Vashchenko, aged 25, and Alexander, her brother who is 22, arrived from the family home in Chernogorsk on Wednesday and later visited Lidiya in the hospital. They accompanied her, with an American diplomat, in the embassy car for the family reunion.

Miss Lubov Vashchenko said Lidiya, Vera, and Alexander had obtained air tickets with the help of United States diplomats and planned to fly to Chernogorsk this morning, earlier than previously planned.

Lubov said the family was very surprised that Soviet authorities allowed the reunion to take place on embassy grounds. She said that American diplomats told her minutes before the meeting that the reunion would have to occur at the compound gate.

Lidiya, on her return to Chernogorsk, plans to apply for permission to emigrate, meeting conditions set by the Soviet authorities.

She said she was convinced the United States government had done all it could to help them. Mrs. Vashchenko told reporters she planned to stop her protest fast after she receives confirmation that Lidiya, Vera, and Alexander are safely back in Chernogorsk.

Lidiya said she was well treated at the hospital and her health was good. However, she said she would start another hunger strike in Chernogorsk if her demand for an exit visa was not met.

Asked if she regarded the reunion as a breakthrough Lubov replied: "I would like to hope, because of the good treatment shown to Lidiya."—AP

12

Routine

We waited with anxiety and hope for news about Lidiya. Within days, a telephone call came through from Chernogorsk. She had reached home safely and would begin preparations to apply for permission to emigrate shortly. Augustina ended her fast, once she knew that her eldest daughter had arrived unharmed. But while one chapter of this extraordinary story was ending, an incident at our home in Chernogorsk was causing me alarm.

While speaking on the telephone with my aunt and sister, I learned that the local officials were preparing documents to draft me into the army. Then on February 8, 1982, officers from the Voenkonat (the military registration and enlistment office) issued a subpoena for me. On March 11, they returned to my home, led by a sergeant named Borisenko.

Although the Soviet authorities had given assurances

that army enlistment would not be compulsory, this proved to be false. Those who refused to serve in the Soviet army were quickly sentenced to a labor camp. Alexander, the eldest son of the Vashchenkos, had already served three years in a labor camp, and at that very moment, Igor Korchnoi, the son of international chess grandmaster Victor Korchnoi, was in a labor camp because he refused to serve in the army. If you do join the army and then apply to emigrate, they can refuse your application stating that you possess "state secrets." If you refuse to serve in the army, they'll arrest you and sentence you to a labor camp.

I found the incident with Borisenko's visit to our family home quite sinister. It showed that the local authorities were preparing documents so that on our return to Chernogorsk, using the pretext of registering our application for an exit visa, they could sentence us all to prison or a labor camp. Previously such incidents passed unnoticed. People like us were subject to the whims of the local officials. But now we had a network of supporters in the West who knew about us. I began to compose an article sharing the latest news with them and requesting them to publicize this information. After a few days, the letter was complete.

I explained that I refused to serve in the army because it was against my religious convictions and my conscience. I said, "Scriptures teach us not to kill and not to take an oath (Matthew 5:21, 34–36). To serve in the army, I would be defending those who repress my parents and people like us."

A few weeks later I was thrilled to notice that my appeal had been distributed among our supporters and published in magazines and newspapers abroad. It also became the focus of an intensive—and very effective—letter-writing campaign. These letters may seem like insignificant and tiny acts, but the Soviet officials really do take notice of such letters and petitions.

Shortly after Lidiya had been put in the hospital, the embassy allowed us to have a second room, Peter, Augustina, Lyuba, and Lilya moved in next door. We became neighbors.

Each of us had our own schedule, and the days followed a kind of routine. We began each day with prayer. We usually prayed several times during the day, always at mealtimes and every night before we slept. Prayer was not a ritual but a vibrant, living experience. It was this communion, above all else, that enabled us to retain our sanity and gave us daily strength.

After breakfast, each of us had different tasks to perform. The women spent a lot of their time doing knitting, sewing, and needlework, some of which they tried to send home to the children; sometimes they gave a shawl or scarf they had knitted to a friend who had been visiting us. Their work was accomplished, and frequently admired by visitors. My time in the morning was spent writing letters and composing appeals to people whom we thought might help, to our friends, and to our supporters. During our stay we wrote letters to many people. Sometimes we received a reply and an encouraging word; at other times, silence.

Together with someone from the consul's office, the women would prepare a shopping list of food items that were needed, and the embassy would deliver our supplies for the week. At first Lilya prepared the food, but after a while this became monotonous for her, so we each took turns cooking for the group. I never found it easy when my turn came. We generally ate salads, rice, boiled vegetables, sausages, and any other kind of meat that was given to us. We also ate a lot of bread and potatoes, the main food in the Soviet Union.

I was able to try all kinds of different recipes, some brought in by visitors who showed us how to prepare and cook the dishes. I like Italian food, especially things like pizza, lasagne, spaghetti Bolognese. Once we tried Japanese food, but this I didn't like; I'm not very adventurous when it comes to trying new food. If we didn't like a new dish or unusual preparation, then we had a problem because we couldn't go out and buy something else from the shops. So the finicky ones usually went to bed hungry. I loved chocolates and sweets, and was always grateful for such gifts from visitors and friends. But after a while, I was unable to eat sweet things because I developed trouble with my teeth and was unable to visit a dentist.

The days were dominated by any developments in our appeal. If we were permitted to speak on the telephone with our family in Chernogorsk, we would walk over to the Consul Section for the call. These telephone calls inevitably affected the rest of the day. After speaking with the family at home, I always felt depressed. I didn't feel like doing anything, just sitting by myself, alone with my thoughts.

If we had visitors, it was a good opportunity to practice English, to find out what was happening among our supporters, and to hear news about our case in the West. Friends also brought us board games, such as scrabble and monopoly, that we played to pass the time. Sometimes news from home was so very bad that we didn't feel like playing or doing anything. At other times, the games were a welcome distraction.

I always enjoyed reading, and the time in the embassy

gave me unlimited opportunities. I found Vladimir Bukovsky's book *To Build a Castle*[46] fascinating. Bukovsky had been imprisoned for twelve years, but his spirit was unbroken. He had a brilliant mind and used his time effectively. He was the first political dissident to be exchanged by the Soviet government when in December 1976 he was exchanged for the Chilean Communist leader Luis Corvalan. Bukovsky took a special interest in our case from the early days and tried to help us. I was deeply touched to receive a postcard from him. It was he who first suggested that we be given work around the embassy to obtain permits from the Moscow authorities for our legal residence in the city. This suggestion was not pursued.

As I was unable to attend school or college, I began studying subjects such as science, history, and mathematics through correspondence courses. Much of my information came from books, magazines, and conversations with people. We had a large map on our wall. Each time we heard of a country from the BBC or Voice of America radio broadcasts or I received a letter from the West, I would check the city's location on the map. This was my geography lesson.

When the embassy staff were leaving Moscow to be posted elsewhere, they would leave some of their clothes for us to wear. I never had any problems about wearing secondhand clothes. I was grateful for everything I received. But when people asked if I wanted a new pair of jeans or something else, my reply was always the same, "I need help with only one thing—emigration."

Some people noticed my stamp collection and the few foreign coins that I had would give me stamps and coins to add to my collection. I gathered signatures from visitors in a small book with blank pages. The book was a reminder of those who passed through my life during these years in the basement. Some visitors declined to write in my book; others quickly filled the page.

I asked one visitor if she had read John Pollock's book about us. She replied "No, and I'm not going to read it. It's a sad story, and I don't like to be reminded of such things. I like cheerful stories with happy endings."

When we were permitted more visitors and people came to know us better, some friends would bring gifts for our birthdays. Then for a brief moment, we were able to forget our predicament and to have a happy time. But I was happiest when we met or heard from people who were praying and working for us. This was the best present I could expect.

Some people thought of us as spiritual heroes. When they discovered that we were actually ordinary mortals with "feet of clay," subject to whims, disagreements, arguments, and opinions, they became disillusioned. Some found it difficult to accept that we quarrelled among ourselves on occasions, that sometimes our opinions were divided, our ideas different. But we numbered seven people from two different families. Each of us was an individual with an imaginative, creative mind. It was natural that our opinions should be individualistic and that our basement should be the center of severe disagreements. But unlike most other families, we couldn't get away from each other to cool off.

I didn't feel that it was necessary to put on a front for our visitors; I didn't want to pretend. We had not chosen this situation, but somehow, here we were. All we could do was remain true to ourselves; all I tried to do was to be myself. I knew that despite everything we experienced together, we were united and bowed before a living God.

On many occasions I found 1 Timothy 4:12 especially encouraging:

> Do not let anyone look down on you because you are young, but be an example for the believers in your speech, your conduct, your love, faith, and purity.

I felt as though the apostle Paul were speaking directly to me. I felt shy because I was so young and because I didn't know English and couldn't always explain what I meant. This verse encouraged me and gave me confidence to try new things.

I also received great encouragement from 2 Corinthians 6:9:

> By our purity, knowledge, patience, and kindness we have shown ourselves to be God's servants.

I knew that many people were praying and working for us. I didn't always know who they were, but from time to time, we would hear about demonstrations, protests, letter-writing campaigns, and many other activities. I tried my best to find out who were organizing projects for us and hoped that someday I could meet them. Gradually we came to know some of the people and organizations who were working for our release. Each time I returned from speaking on the telephone with one of our supporters, I would check the map on the wall. As the months passed, the places to identify increased: Alabama, New York, Dublin, Andijk, Zurich, Dallas, Amsterdam, Paris, Stockholm, Seattle, Washington, Hilversum, London, St. Louis, Manchester, and Wheaton.

13

Peace, Peace

I read the article slowly, tracing each line with my finger. It was good practice for my English; I learned many new words, checking the dictionary for some of the longer ones.

This article from a current news magazine was about the emerging Peace Movement in the West with demonstrations and marches attended by thousands of people. The protests were supported by politicians, clergymen, and people from all age groups. The article stated that the greatest issue of modern times was the threat of nuclear war. One statesman was quoted as saying, "Mankind now has in its power the capacity to totally annihilate planet Earth. Nuclear weapons have reduced the war game to an art form."

It was interesting to read magazines such as *Time* and *Newsweek* and to compare them with the Soviet press. I realized that all publications reflect some bias, but at least the events were covered and not totally ignored, as was the case in the Soviet publications. The Soviet newspapers also contained articles about peace, and their theme was always the same: "The Soviets want peace; the Americans want war. We have to defend ourselves." It was curious for me to learn how many Western peace groups seemed to echo this view.

The Soviet press does not report demonstrations inside the USSR. There aren't any. If such protests do occur, they are organized by the authorities. Spontaneous activity is quickly and decisively curtailed. The leaders of an independent "peace" group in the USSR have been forced to break up. Some have been arrested; others expelled. People here understand that if they try to organize a demonstration for peace, they'll end up in prison. No one is fooled by the Soviet's rhetoric about peace. They realize that the Soviets want power not peace to dominate the world. Usually people keep quiet because they have enough problems, and don't want any more. They don't want to lose their jobs or a chance for a promotion nor do they want to face discrimination because of their views.

There are regular lectures about the peaceful intentions of the Soviet Union. We must arm ourselves if we want peace, is the general theme. "Kill for peace" some people joke. Factory workers are encouraged to work harder "for peace" and on many occasions, such as Lenin's Day, they are "invited" to donate their day's wages "to the cause." Donations are collected regularly from the workers and in April, they honor "The Unknown Soldier" with such collections. A standing joke among factory workers goes like this:

Question: If you had the power to raise one man from the dead, who would you choose? Lenin? Jesus? Who else?

Answer: The Unknown Soldier!

Can the issues of peace and justice be separated? Clearly it's impossible to have one without the other. Vladimir Bukovsky understands this only too well. In 1979, he published a letter in *Time* magazine, in support of our case. He wrote:

> It is a dangerous myth that the fate of others has nothing to do with our own . . . more is at stake than the lives of two families. At the very least, should not the Soviets be required to honor past international agreements respecting emigration and human rights before we sign new ones with them? Let the Soviets demonstrate their good faith and allow these Christians (and all others who wish it) to emigrate.[47]

Bukovsky published a booklet entitled *The Peace Movement and the Soviet Union* in which he explains the Soviet infiltration of peace groups in the West and the Communist government's true intentions.[48]

It was Lenin, who put it quite simply: "As an ultimate objective, peace simply means Communist world control."

Perhaps some sincere people are convinced by the slogans of peace. But slogans are insufficient evidence, as the Old Testament prophet Jeremiah cries: "From the least to the greatest all are greedy for gain; prophets and priests alike, all practice deceit. They dress the wound of my people as though it were not serious. 'Peace, peace,' they say, when there is no peace."[49]

Unfortunately many peace groups in the West share the same objectives as the government of the Soviet Union. In the foreword to Bukovsky's book, the British MP Winston Churchill pointed out, "In 1981 alone, Soviet 'diplomats' or 'news correspondents' had to be expelled from Norway,

Denmark, and the Netherlands for secretly funding local 'peace' movements."

Bukovsky points out another classic campaign for peace from the not-too-distant past. In a secret address to the German press in Munich on November 10, 1938, Adolf Hitler stated:

> The prevailing circumstances have obliged me to speak, for a decade or more, of almost nothing but peace. Only, in fact, by continuously declaring the German desire for peace and Germany's peaceful intentions was I able, step by step, to secure freedom for the German people and to provide Germany with the armaments which have, time and time again, always been the essential preconditions for any future move.[50]

We should not be fooled. Rather we should be careful to learn from such men as Alexandr Solzhenitsyn. When Solzhenitsyn visited London for the first time in March 1976, he talked with the BBC and his words have even greater significance now than they did then.

> I think there is no such thing as detente. Detente is necessary, but detente with open hands. Show that there is no stone in your hands. But your partners with whom you are conducting detente have a stone in their hands, and it is so heavy that it could kill you with one single blow. Detente becomes self-deception; that's what it is all about.[51]

The Soviets have been quick to seize every opportunity in the propaganda war. One strategy has been to use the religious audiences, and many Soviet churchmen have been paraded in the West espousing the Soviet government's commitment to peace. The Soviets scored a major publicity scoop in 1982 when many Western churchmen attended a "Peace Conference" in Moscow organized by the Russian Orthodox church. Clearly some leaders feel that dialogue is necessary, even obligatory, if there is to be change. But if the sacrifice of principles is the price we must pay, then I question such action.

The Peace Conference offered Western Christians a chance to telegram a message to the church-in-chains and their captors. Instead, many chose to attend, blithely assuming that another channel would be cleared for "communication." The star attraction at this conference was the attendance of Dr. Billy Graham for what was "virtually the keynote address of the congress," although he was not strictly a delegate.

It is widely accepted that if the West is strong in such circumstances, small victories can be won from the Soviets by securing the release of some prisoners. But how would those Christians in prisons, psychiatric hospitals, and labor camps react upon hearing the news that Western Christians were arriving in Moscow to discuss "peace?"

Nearly five hundred religious leaders from eighty nations attended the conference, and the proceedings were hosted by the Russian Orthodox church. Religious dissidents in Moscow were warned directly and indirectly not to get near the conference or to make contact with the visitors. There were twenty-one arrests and fifty house searches— all April 6. Vasily Barats was picked up by the KGB and held in a psychiatric clinic for a two-day examination where he was asked about his plans for the days of the conference. He said later, "They told me very simply to stay away or I would be kept away, if not in a hospital then in jail."[52]

For some time it was debatable whether Billy Graham would attend the conference. When it was known that he had accepted, not as a delegate, hopes were high among some that he would use his influence to secure our release. In an article in the *Church of England Newspaper*, the Reverend Michael Bourdeaux wrote, "Clearly Billy Graham faces one of the greatest challenges of his career. He could still say to the Patriarch of the Russian Orthodox church, 'I need the emigration of the Siberian Seven and their families as a very small gesture before I finally appear in your pulpit.' "[53]

Dr. Graham's comments have been widely reported, and he has claimed that the problems surrounding his visit to Moscow were caused by misunderstandings arising from the secular Western press correspondents in Moscow. He said he was misquoted. I will only repeat here one comment that he made. When asked, "Did you personally see any evidence of religious persecution?" He replied to the question, "No, I personally did not see any evidence of religious persecution."

I thought about that reply for a long time. If I had not lived in the embassy basement for four years as a result of persecution, why else had I stayed here? And it was, in fact, in the embassy that I met Dr. Billy Graham.

14

The Most Unusual Visit

In the embassy in Moscow, I met many different kinds of people—ambassadors, senators, even the vice-president of the United States, also ordinary people from many different parts of the world. But the most unusual visitor was Dr. Billy Graham. I had heard about Dr. Graham in Chernogorsk and had seen his articles and books. In the Soviet Union, he was held in very high regard.

When he arrived in the Moscow airport, one of the foreign correspondents asked him about Lyuba Vashchenko's appeal to him to help resolve her family's case. Dr. Graham replied that he was unaware of her letter, whereupon the correspondent produced a copy of it and handed it to the American evangelist.[54]

After this incident at the airport, the correspondents continued to ask him about our case. At first he said he would not meet with us, but some time during his stay in

Moscow he changed his mind. Before his visit, his aides came to our basement to discuss with us the conditions under which he would visit us. There were many conditions: the curtains would have to be drawn during his stay; our talk must remain secret, not to be discussed with anyone including correspondents. These discussions lasted about one and a half hours. Nevertheless, we were still pleased to see Dr. Graham when he finally arrived. I had written a letter addressed to him and handed it to him when he arrived (see Appendix I). I asked him if he would help us, and he replied, "I will pray for you."

I was surprised that he said he would pray for us but couldn't commit himself to doing anything. Even ordinary people, without any influence, had said they would try, at least, to petition the Soviet authorities. He was not an ordinary person, and more importantly, he actually had contact with the authorities. When others in the room asked him about trying to resolve our case, he said, "I talked with Soviet officials. I hope they will resolve this problem." We tried to find out a little more about this. He replied again, "I hope they will resolve this problem."

From that sentence I understood him to mean that it was "his hope" that the Soviets would resolve our case. He had talked to them and mentioned us, but to whom, we didn't know. He then said, "I came to preach not to get involved with any political issues."

I was surprised to hear this. We were Christians who were fighting for our freedom after both our families had suffered at the hands of the Soviet authorities. Sometimes we were in peril of our lives. Ours was a religious problem, not a political issue, so what was the problem about meeting with us?

Billy Graham claimed that the Western press misquoted

him. I wonder what he thought of the passing reference to our case in a Radio Moscow broadcast on August 4, 1982 about "Religious Freedom." The commentator Boris Botlisky stated:

> I could cite no evidence on the extent of religious freedom that exists in this country, but since this evidence coming from me and from Radio Moscow might seem suspect to you, for that very reason I will instead quote the testimony of unimpeachable witnesses. The latest of these has been the American evangelist Dr. Billy Graham, whom no one in his right mind would suspect of sympathizing with the Soviet system. Now at the conclusion of his visit to the Soviet Union earlier this summer, Billy Graham said he had found more religious freedom in the Soviet Union than in Britain, with its established Church of England. Here are Billy Graham's exact words: "I think there is a lot more freedom here than the impression that has been given in the States, because there are hundreds or even thousands of churches open. In Great Britain they have a state church, in other countries you have state churches, here the church is not a state church, it's a free church."

The broadcast continued in this vein, quoting other Western clergymen, and then stated, "In Britain, Keston College in particular is, alas, notorious for thus falsifying the status of religion in this country."[55]

If Dr. Graham came to preach, to whom did he preach? One report in the *International Herald Tribune* estimated that one third of his audience would have been carefully selected state officials. On the Sunday of his visit, he was to have spoken at the Orthodox church in the morning and the Baptist church in the evening. Sensing that there might be some disturbances, at the last moment the officials rescheduled the Baptist church's evening service to about eight o'clock in the morning.

Undeterred, many Christians still arrived outside the church but were unable to get in. These people had come from all over the Soviet Union to see Dr. Graham. They held an impromptu service in the street and were not disturbed by the militia—an unprecedented move.

During the service, one young lady held up a banner listing the number of Baptist prisoners "for the work of the gospel." A young man held up a sign "Deliver those who are drawn away to death." A third woman tried to raise another sign, but a man in plain clothes ripped it from her hands.[56] For a long time I wondered who the girl in the Baptist church might have been and what happened to her. I never heard about her again. I hope some people will continue to pray for her and try to help her.

I heard many reasons for Dr. Graham's words and actions during his visit to Moscow. One was that the Soviet authorities had granted his last wish: to preach in the USSR. For this, he was necessarily cautious about his every move, so he would not offend the authorities. In my opinion the Soviet government enticed Dr. Graham with the possibility of preaching in the Moscow stadium and used his visit to their advantage.

Before he left our basement, Dr. Graham read from the Scriptures and shared some of his thoughts about the passage with us. He then presented each of us with a pen, with his signature, and with two books. Lyuba Vashchenko asked if he would take a family photograph with them for their private album. He agreed, but then his aides forbade it.

After our meeting, I was surprised to hear him ask the consul how he could escape without meeting the press who had been waiting around the embassy building for an interview. The consul replied that he would help but that Dr. Graham would have to speak to them for a few minutes. This he agreed to do, and he called our meeting a "pastoral visit."

I read some of his comments concerning his visit. Later he said that he had been misquoted. It's true that his visit to the Soviet Union was surrounded with controversy, both in the Christian world and in the media world wide. There are many opinions about what he should have said or done. I can only speak from where I was—stuck in the American Embassy.

For me, it was the strangest and most disappointing visit of all the visits to our basement home.

15

Think—Don't Think

Mr. George Bush, vice-president of the United States, smiled and shook my hand. "You're almost as tall as I am," he said jokingly. Standing at his side was Mr. George Schultz, secretary of state. He also smiled as we shook hands. The tiny basement room looked crowded as both men sat in our midst.

Mr. Bush and Mr. Schultz were among the world leaders who were attending the funeral of Leonid Brezhnev.

I was quite surprised when they decided to visit us: a few years ago this would not have seemed possible. Their visit indicated a high degree of support by the American government for our case. It was inconceivable that the Soviet authorities would not have noted the event.

It was a brief meeting, but they appeared sympathetic. They posed for photographs with us and both signed my autograph book. As they were leaving Mr. Schultz said, "We'll try to help you if we can."

"Yes," Mr. Bush added. "Don't give up hope."

Joseph Stalin became the Communist Party leader in 1922. After his death in 1953, Gregori Malenkov briefly held the post; then came Nikita Khrushchev. Leonid Brezhnev took over in 1964. I didn't mourn for Mr. Brezhnev. He was a powerful man who ruled over an evil empire. If he had repented and turned to God, he could have changed the course of history.

He was replaced by Yuri Andropov, the previous head of the dreaded KGB. Andropov was the man responsible for the persecution of many Christians and Jews, the expulsion of Solzhenitsyn, the exile of Sakharov, and the imprisonment of many innocent people.

The KGB is known as the eyes and ears of the Soviet Union. They have agents and informers everywhere. Some KGB agents are especially trained at "Bible Studies" Institutes to try to convince Christians to reject their faith. Only strong Communists are sent to these institutes; those whom they hope will fight for communism until death. Perhaps the KGB are afraid that some agents will be converted after studying the Bible, and so they are very cautious. Those who graduate are valuable to the state. They can be used to infiltrate the church in the USSR and can also impress Western church leaders when they visit. It's not uncommon to meet a KGB agent who knows the Bible better than many Christians.

While in the embassy, I read Western newspapers and magazines for the first time. I was surprised by the freedom of the media and by the power such a force clearly had. Reports were published, no matter how scandalous that delved into intimate and personal details about people's lives, and they were sometimes based merely on unconfirmed rumors. There were almost "no limits" in some articles and no subject that had not been laid bare in glossy full-color photographs.

Life in the Soviet Union is so very, very different. Newspapers are very cheap. A two-page paper would cost about two kopeks, a four-page paper four kopeks, and so forth. There are two major newspapers in the Soviet Union: *Pravda* and *Izvestiya*. Both are controlled by the Kremlin and serve to impart official doctrine and policy. *Pravda* means "truth" and *Izvestiya* is translated as "news." There is a longstanding joke that says everyone knows there's no news in the Truth and no truth in the News. Every single word that appears in both these papers has been checked and double checked many times by the censors before approval is given for publication.

It is impossible to understand what life in the Soviet Union is like without comprehending the phenomenon of censorship. Almost no criticism of the country is permitted in any form whatsoever. And everything everywhere is under official control. The late Arkady Belinkov stated that censorship practiced in the USSR is a new phenomenon in the history of thought control. Think—don't think.

Solzhenitsyn was arrested in February 1945 for criticizing Stalin in letters to a friend. Years later he would remember his arrest and recollect, "They arrested me because of my naivety. I knew it was forbidden to mention military secrets in letters from the front, but I thought thinking was legitimate."

Lenin visualized the press as twenty-six lead soldiers, a force fulfilling three main functions: It was to be a "collective organizer, propagandist, and agitator." And this principle is still the guiding force today. Any fact that might not aid the interests of the party must be suppressed, whatever its news value; sometimes because of it.

Stalin once said that the role of the press in a socialist society was to be that of a state advertising agency. Consequently, the need for censorship is a necessity. The office of censorship was never introduced formally by law, but instituted in a clandestine way in inner party instructions. It's said that over 70,000 individual censors control the newspapers, magazines, and publishers. To aid them in their job, the state publishes a book listing everything that is not allowed to be mentioned in print without specific permission. The book is titled *Index of Information Not to Be Published in the Open Press*.[57]

The *Index* forbids a variety of items:

Accidents involving aircrafts, ships, automobiles.

Consequences of earthquakes, tidal waves, floods, and other natural calamities.

Labor camps or "information about extraordinary events in the camps such as suicides and illnesses."

The opening or closing of churches and the number of churchgoers.

In his book *The KGB,* John Barron reports that Leonid Finkelstein, once an editor of a leading scientific journal, was asked to delete a figure denoting the diameter of the earth. "Has this become a secret, too?" Finkelstein asked.

"Yes," replied the censor. "There is a directive not to publish the exact size of the planet."[58]

When Solzhenitsyn submitted the manuscript of *August 1914* for publication, the censors found a problem with the word "God" that was written in capitals, and it was suggested that the word be written in lower case. When the author refused, the book was banned. *August 1914* was the first book Solzhenitsyn publicly authorized for publication in the West.

Such censorship employed on a large scale can easily be

used to play tricks with the mind. In *The KGB,* John Barron provides documentation of two classic incidents of Soviet manipulation, made possible through the climate of censorship already present. The cases may be old but are worth retelling.

Sir John Maynard, a British agricultural expert, went on an OGPU guided tour of the Ukraine at the height of the 1932-33 famine that, according to Robert Conquest's calculations, took five to six million lives. Back in London, Maynard assured the world there was no famine, isolated food scarcities perhaps, but certainly no widespread hunger. Similarly, George Bernard Shaw returned from an OGPU tour to report that there was no evidence of starvation. After all, he noted, the hotels where he dined abounded with food.[59]

The second case worth noting concerns one of Stalin's concentration camps. In 1944, two distinguished Americans—Henry A. Wallace, the vice-president, and Professor Owen Latimore, representing the Office of War Information—visited Dalstroy, a camp in the gold-mining region of Siberia. Dalstroy housed many political prisoners and was considered to be one of the most barbarous camps where prisoners were routinely clubbed, beaten, or in many thousands of cases, shot. The annual mortality rate in the mine was thirty percent, and Robert Conquest concluded that between 1937 and 1941 alone, at least a million Dalstroy prisoners perished.

The night before the American visitors arrived, the NKVD (now known as the KGB) personnel dismantled the camp watchtowers and from private stocks filled the shelves with Soviet goods. Barron notes:

The emaciated women prisoners who toiled as swine at the nearby farm were replaced by the most presentable NKVD women available. Strong, healthy, happy young men showed up in the mines to relieve the gaunt prisoners. During the three days the Americans visited the camps, all prisoners were kept out of sight under guard, and for the first and last time, shown motion pictures so they would create no disturbances.[60]

Such eclipses are evident today in modern Soviet society, though subtlety and tact play an increasingly important role. Secrecy and intrigue still characterize the Kremlin. There are many examples. Yuri Andropov was dead before the world knew he had a living wife, noted *Time* magazine in its wrap-up article about the KGB chief turned party boss. Speculation about his successor's health—Konstantin Chernenko was seventy-three when he took over—stemmed from television shots of Andropov's funeral when viewers saw the new leader's inability to raise or extend his right arm.

The KGB still plays a key role in fulfilling the Soviet government's obsession with secrecy and enforcing surveillance as a way of life. Telephone calls to all parts of the Soviet Union must be cleared through the central Moscow operator. Inevitably these calls are monitored. Every time I spoke on the telephone—whether to our family in Chernogorsk or to our friends in America and England—I expected the KGB to be listening in on our conversation.

Similarly, the international mail is sorted through a central clearing office in Moscow. The KGB have a machine that screens all mail. Any letters that we received in the embassy had been checked. Sometimes if they are unable to read a single line, they confiscate the entire letter.

In the Soviet Union, there is a presumption of guilt. This creates a natural suspicion among people, even within families. At times, the entire system is like a chess board, full of unsuspecting pawns, providing evidence of your guilt. Many people in the judicial system are ashamed at the lack of evidence or the contradictory evidence in some cases involving Jews, Christian believers, and dissidents, but they are reluctant to take a stand against such corruption because of fear of the KGB.

There is a bitter joke that goes like this. One of the Kremlin leaders lost his cigarette lighter and asked the KGB to look into the matter. The lighter was soon found, so the leader telephoned the KGB and asked how the investigation was going.

The KGB chief said, "We've already arrested ten men and new leads are coming in every minute."

The man in the Kremlin replied, "Oh, but I have already found my lighter, so there must be a mistake."

The KGB said in a startled voice, "But Minister, seven of them have already confessed."

16

The Longest Day

Days turned to months and then years. In 1978, we spent anxious moments fearful of being evicted at any moment. Four years later, I began to wonder if we would ever leave. It was difficult to predict what the Soviet authorities were thinking. We dared to hope. Every time we heard of a new initiative in our case we prayed a breakthrough might follow. But each approach was met with a stone wall of silence.

In Chernogorsk, the authorities played a cat-and-mouse game with little indication of any change. Lidiya Vashchenko had not received permission to emigrate. On November 25, my father, Katharina, and other believers were summoned to the OVIR. The director told them that the Moscow OVIR had sent a document stating that we had all been denied emigration because we had no relatives abroad. When my father asked for a copy of this document, the director said her instructions were to explain it orally.

I found it hard to believe that December would mark our fourth Christmas in the embassy. So much had happened. We spent the day in prayer and fasting.

My English had improved, slightly, and I spent a few days early in December composing a "Christmas letter" to our friends in the West. I wrote:

> Dear Friends, we wish you a Merry Christmas and that God will help you in your lives so that you will continue to intercede for those who are repressed for their faith in God.
>
> In my Christmas letter, I wish to turn to people of my age with the plea to help me to be free and, like you, freely worship our Lord and Creator Jesus Christ.
>
> Dear parents, I turn to you with a petition both to the governments of the USA and the USSR to resolve our family's problem. Just as you desire happiness and joy for your own children, I ask you to please help me to be happy and joyful in your country just as your children are. I want to freely follow God's teachings unafraid that I will be repressed.

Some things had changed—improved, some may argue. But were we any nearer getting exit visas from the Soviet government? I really didn't know.

And so we lived, as day followed day.

And then . . . I couldn't believe it was true. I was so shocked by the news, I couldn't move. Lidiya Vashchenko had received an exit visa! Within a few hours, she would be in the West!

Free!

After fourteen months at home in Chernogorsk, the impossible had happened. Anxiously we waited for news and confirmation.

On April 6, 1983, at five-forty in the afternoon Lidiya

arrived in Vienna, Austria. A few hours later, she placed a telephone call to the American Embassy and talked with her sister Lyuba and other members of her family. Yes, it was true. This was no Soviet trick. It really was Lidiya. She really was in the West.

Free! Free at last!

A tremendous feeling of excitement seemed to grip us. The prayer and action of thousands of people all over the world had been answered. The deadlock in the Vashchenkos' case had been broken with Lidiya's precious exit visa. I was so happy for the Vashchenko family. They now had a close relative abroad. If the Soviet government wanted, they could issue visas to the rest of the Vashchenkos for "family reunification."

Lidiya flew from Vienna to Israel. At Tel Aviv's airport virtually the entire corps of foreign media correspondents had come to report her arrival.

"We have always believed God was calling us to go to Israel," *Time* magazine quoted her as saying. Lidiya's arrival in Israel was one step in the fulfillment of the Vashchenkos' twenty-two-year struggle.

Lidiya's emigration did not affect us. We were the Chmykhalovs, a different family. We had no one in the West.

Because the Soviets usually permit visas for Israel, this seemed to provide the best opportunity for our emigration. That's what everyone thought. Even President Reagan. Again the pressure began for us to leave the embassy and return home. But was this another trick to get us to leave the basement? What hope did we really have of getting exit visas without any family member in the West?

Some correspondents had written that we thought we could be whisked out of the country by helicopter, commando-style. But I knew we would have to leave the embassy, possibly return home, and travel to the airport to leave. But in that decision was a tremendous risk.

Papa and Vladimir arrived in Moscow to visit us. The joy of seeing them once again was mixed with tension. Although we each had questions about the past, the time was spent trying to decide the future. What should we do? Nothing happens in the Soviet Union by accident. How were we to interpret Lidiya Vashchenko's emigration? Trying to unravel the meaning of Soviet actions and policy is like attempting to get out of a maze blindfolded.

After receiving a telephone call from Lidiya in Israel, the Vashchenko family had decided to leave the embassy and return home. They were next door collecting their few belongings together. Mama decided to return with them. Papa and Vladimir were pleased, but a cloud of concern still remained. Should I return with them? What would happen if I left the embassy? Would I be arrested? Would I be forced to join the army? Who would help us if we were harassed by local officials? Would we be able to communicate with the embassy and correspondents in Moscow? How could we keep in touch with our supporters in the West? Would people forget about us? On the other hand, how could I remain in the embassy? How could I stay in Moscow and watch my family returning home without me?

I was so confused that it was hard to focus and view events in perspective. Everything seemed unreal; the dangers were amplified. The world beyond the embassy gates was dark and sinister. This was the longest day of my life.

Prayer is communion with God. It's not dependent on the length of time spent on our knees or the eloquence and choice of words. Rather, it's the attitude of our hearts that is important. We usually begin and end our prayers with the word "Lord." In this way we are acknowledging Jesus as Lord of our life and accepting that we are servants.

God doesn't always answer our prayers for peace with tranquility and peace of mind. He doesn't always give us exactly what we want, sometimes because we don't know what's best.

Of course, God, in His sovereignty, grants special requests very specially. Time and again, I have been given the exact thing I requested, but at other times there seems no answer from the Lord. We are not puppets, and prayer is not magic. This single thing that God desires to give His children is the gift of trust. When in difficulties, when the times seem too troubled and out of control, when the complexities of life seem out of the reach of men's solutions, then our prayers should request that gift of trusting God. It is man's highest calling.

The time had come to leave the sanctuary of the American Embassy. It was our best chance of being allowed to emigrate. The risks were frightening. Confused, tired, almost beyond despair, I began to pray. *Lord, I trust you. . . .*

17

Return

I stood at the gate of our home and watched the people go by. It was such a strange feeling, standing outside. I walked down the street, not really sure of where I was going, just walking. It felt so good. This small act of freedom and choice seemed a luxury.

Chernogorsk hadn't changed much. There were new buildings, some ten stories high. Some of the older houses had a fresh coat of paint. The television news still reported a full harvest and factories at top productivity. In Chernogorsk, the shops were still empty.

There was a lot of news to catch up on. So much had happened in the last five years. Some of my childhood friends had married and moved away. Our dog had died. And yet some things seemed to have stood still.

"I've got a surprise for you, Timothy," Anatoly said. He spoke shyly, standing in the doorway. "There's someone I want you to meet." He moved backward and reached behind the door. Standing beside him was a dark-haired girl, pretty and petite. She looked shy and awkward. "Don't be embarrassed," Anatoly told her.

"Hello," I said. Walking up to her, I extended my hand quite formally. "I'm Timothy, the 'American' from Moscow."

"Yes," she said, "I recognized you from the photographs I've seen. My name is Svetlana."

We walked on to the porch of our home and continued talking. The sun was sinking, and soon it would be night. I asked Anatoly how long they had known each other.

"We met in church," Anatoly replied, "about two years ago."

Svetlana was specific. "It was October, four months before my seventeenth birthday."

They told me that during the last two years they had become close friends. "We're praying about getting married, Timothy."

It took a moment for the news to register. I jumped up and hugged both of them. I was so pleased for Anatoly. He had found a lovely Christian girl who would support and help him through life. As we were talking, Alexander returned home. He was fortunate to have found work as a driver. After drinking tea together the four of us walked down to our eldest brother's home.

Vladimir and Katharina lived closeby. They had married in October 1977, one year before we went to Moscow. Because Vladimir didn't have a passport, the Soviet authorities refused to register their marriage officially. They did have a church wedding, but all four of the children were forced to take their mother's maiden name of Ruts. At first Roman, Yelena, Svetlana, and Vladimir were shy but soon made friends with me, and we spent an enjoyable evening together as we talked about the past four years. Life had not been easy for them while we were in the embassy. There were problems, as in all families.

On Sunday we all gathered together for the church services, and I met more of my old friends. Many Christians had faced great hardships and persecution, but none of these things had weakened the body of believers. Despite the problems, I noticed many new Christians in our local church. There is no force on earth greater than the power of God. No matter how hard men try to destroy faith, they will find it a struggle that they can never win.

In many of the factories, Christians are often mocked and humiliated. They are given the worst jobs, the lowest wages, and the longest hours. They are the butt of all jokes. Sometimes they are asked to speak while everyone stands around joking and making fun of them. The Christian workers view this as an opportunity to witness for their faith. After they speak, some of their fellow workers come secretly to them and ask questions about God. This is an opportunity for the Holy Spirit to work.

It's very dangerous to share your faith in the Soviet Union. If the police or the KGB find out, both you and those you've talked to about Christianity will lose privileges and opportunities at work and in the community; the chance of promotion will be limited; your children will not be allowed to enter colleges of further education; perhaps you may be fired from your job.

The state is the only employer in the Soviet Union. If you are fired from one place, it's difficult to find another job, although generally there is plenty of employment. In the Soviet Union, production and demand form an unhappy marriage. Winter goods may be delayed by slow production and only arrive in the shops in summer. Similarly, new designs in sports shirts may only be released in winter, a time wholly unsuitable for the products. Most people have learned to buy what they need when they see it, since they may never see it again.

Once we needed tomato paste for cooking, but we had to wait one and a half months before it became available. Then it was sold in three liter cans. Without thinking about it, we bought three cans, not knowing when it would be on the shelves again. It is best if you know somebody who is a manager in a store or employed in one of the shops. This way you learn ahead of time when things will become available and stand a better chance of buying and beating the long lines. There is, of course, a thriving black market, which provides everything you can imagine. Blue jeans and rock records are always on top of the list.

I telephoned the American Embassy in Moscow regularly to keep in touch. Despite the many friends that tried to telephone us, only one call came through—Jane Drake in Alabama. I knew we had not been forgotten, but when I actually heard her voice, it was a tremendous encouragement. A verse of Scripture came to mind: "Like cold water to a weary soul is good news from a distant land" (Proverbs 25:25, NIV).

18

Whirlwind Romance

Not all our friends had moved away. While in the embassy, I often thought about one of my friends back in Chernogorsk, a young girl named Tatyana Plotnikova, whom I had met as a teenager. Tatyana and her two sisters Nadezhda and Galina lived with their mother Alexandra Plotnikova in the same suburb of Chernogorsk as we did.

Tatyana had worked as a crane operator in a factory where they made concrete products. She was extremely skilled with her hands and also an adept carpenter. She used to work a late-night shift, four in the afternoon to midnight, so I would meet her after work and escort her home. As we walked, we discussed many different things. The stars above provided quite a romantic setting, and I found myself increasingly wooed by her charm and unassuming nature. Had I been more forward, I would have realized that I was a teenager in love. I merely thought of myself as a secret admirer.

During my stay in the embassy, I sometimes imagined myself strolling by her side, but I never knew if that chance would come. Plucking up courage, I mailed her a Christmas card in 1979, trusting it would get through the postal surveillance.

To my surprise and delight, she replied. She wrote many letters to me telling me about her life and what was happening in Chernogorsk and in the local church. Some of her letters were read by Soviet officials and were confiscated.

Now that I was home, I decided to surprise Tatyana with an impromptu visit, and so one day I walked over to her house. She already knew that we had decided to leave the embassy and that we would be returning to our hometown, but she had no idea when. I hoped that she would run up, throw her arms around me, and kiss me, but being shy, she restrained herself.

"I'm so happy to see you again, Timothy," she said.

We talked for a while, and as I was leaving, I asked if I could see her again. Tatyana was busy remodeling her home with the help of her sisters. I visited her home every day after that. She was busy sawing and hammering; I pitched in and helped. Soon an extra room had been added to the house. In between the carpentry work during some extended "tea breaks" for the "workers," we talked a lot together.

After ten days had passed, I plucked up all my courage, took a deep breath, and asked Tatyana if she would marry me. It was April 28 when I proposed, and she accepted me. It was the most beautiful time of my life. I just couldn't stop smiling.

Two days later, I celebrated my twenty-first birthday. A few friends and family members gathered together, and

Tatyana baked a special cake for me. When Tatyana agreed to marry me, it was the best birthday present I could have hoped to receive.

According to Soviet law, if you wish to marry, you are required to register with the civil authorities known as ZAGS and submit your application to them. A date is appointed whereupon you must return to officially register the marriage. The day we were given was Friday, June 17, 1983.

The law also states that one week before official registration, the couple must return to ZAGS and confirm the details of the marriage with the officials. So on June 10, Tatyana and I reported to the office stating our intention to proceed with the wedding. During this meeting the officials found something suspicious about our application, and they asked Tatyana to leave the room because they wished to speak with me privately. I wanted to go with her, but they blocked my path to the exit. Reluctantly, I sat down.

Then the officials began to discourage me from marrying my lovely Tatyana. They said, "What if you and your family receive permission to emigrate from the Soviet Union, won't you want to leave with them? This girl will not receive permission. You will be in the West, and she will be here in Siberia. She will never receive permission to emigrate."

I realized that this might be a problem, but Tatyana and I were in love. I couldn't bear the thought of leaving her behind in Chernogorsk if we did receive exit visas.

I knew also that life in the West was very different. Many exiles and emigrants found it hard to adjust and to cope with the pressures and pace of life. But Tatyana had shared my past; a Siberian wife would think and feel the same as I. We knew the coming years would be difficult, but our strength would come from being together. The time to take a wife was now.

I prayed and asked God to make it possible for Tatyana to leave the Soviet Union with our family. I also telephoned the American Embassy in Moscow to inform them of my decision to marry and if her name could be included on an invitation from the West.[61]

At the end of June, the Vashchenkos received the news for which they had waited twenty-two years: *exit visas!* I felt strangely elated, almost as though I were going to leave with them. I wished them good-by at Chernogorsk's railway station where they caught a train to Moscow. We had been through so much together, but the struggle had not been in vain.

I remained on the platform for a few minutes after the train left, feeling somewhat disconsolate and empty. It was a bittersweet feeling I couldn't exactly put into words. I didn't know if I would ever see them again.

On June 27, 1983, fifteen members of the Vashchenko family arrived in Vienna, five years to the exact day that our ordeal had begun outside the American Embassy in Moscow.

But what was to become of our family?

The days in Chernogorsk were uneventful. No one from the army registration office had visited our home with draft papers for me. The police didn't follow up the case against Papa. Neither had the KGB or the militia showed any particular interest in us. We were ignored.

19

"Don't Get Lost Again in Moscow"

Early in July, Tatyana and I decided to enjoy a short holiday together. Her elder sister Galina accompanied us, as we traveled to a few places visiting friends. On Monday, July 11, we arrived in Moscow. It was early morning, about three o'clock. We thought we would spend a few days sightseeing in Moscow before deciding whether we would return to Chernogorsk directly or travel further. After breakfast at the railway station, I telephoned the American Embassy and spoke to Wayne Leininger, the U.S. consul. He agreed to meet us in a nearby park at one o'clock. This meant that we had a few hours free, but we were quite tired from the traveling. We strolled over to the park, found a shady spot, and dozed in the noonday sun.

The consul was punctual, and we talked for a while. Several times during our conversation, I noticed a man in the park keeping a close eye on our little group. After our conversation, the consul left, but we remained where we were because we had arranged to meet some other friends from the embassy at the same spot.

An elderly lady walked past us, and two policemen approached her and stopped to examine her papers. The man who had been observing our meeting with the consul walked over to the trio. Galina, Tatyana, and I strolled to the notice board near the street exit of the park and pretended to read the papers pinned on the board. From the corner of my eye, I saw that they had finished with the lady and were heading in our direction. I whispered to Tatyana and Galina to follow me, and we turned and headed directly toward them.

"We want to check your documents," one of the policemen addressed me politely as we passed alongside each other.

"Why?" I replied. "There are many people in the park. Why don't you check their papers?"

"No, no," he said quickly, slightly embarrassed. "We checked the documents of that lady there. Didn't you see us doing that?"

I had all our documents so I handed them over to the policeman. "From which city have you come?" he inquired.

"You can see from the documents," I replied, in a matter-of-fact tone.

"What are you doing here?" he asked casually looking through the documents and internal passports.

"We've come to see Moscow. We've never seen the city."

He then asked where we were staying and how long we would remain in the city. I replied that we had plane tickets but that all the flights to Chernogorsk were full. All this time, a KGB man who was with the policemen remained silent. Now he beckoned me to one side. "I want to talk to you alone," he said.

Tatyana replied, "If you've got something to say, then speak to both of us."

The man whispered quietly to me so the policemen couldn't hear. "Your father wants to find you very quickly. He's been searching for you and your wife."

I was puzzled by his words. It was the first time I had heard Tatyana referred to as my wife. Although we had registered our marriage by Soviet law, we had not had a Christian marriage in church.

The KGB man asked, "Are you waiting for anyone else?"

Then I realized that they must have been listening in on our telephone conversation that morning. Not only did they know where to find us, but they also knew we had planned to meet someone else. He spoke slowly and insinuatingly. "Are you sure you won't get lost again in Moscow?"

I understood the hint immediately. He knew I had been lost for nearly five years in Moscow.

"You don't have a lot of time. You have to hurry. If you like, I can help you with tickets to return to Chernogorsk."

Once again, I was very surprised by his words. It was the first time in my life that the KGB had ever tried actually to help us.

"Come," he said, "I have my car parked right here with my own driver. I'm sure we can find some spare seats on the plane for you."

As we walked toward the exit of the park, one policeman walked with us, another with the KGB man. The policeman beside us said, "What did the KGB man want with you? What were you talking about?"

175

I replied, "You don't know? How strange it is that you don't know. After all, you came with him. Why don't you ask him?"

His car was a black Volga. We climbed into the back seat, and he sat in front with his driver. I was a little nervous because this was the first time that I had dealt— alone—with the KGB.

"May I know your name?" I asked.

"No, no, you've seen me before," he replied enigmatically. I couldn't understand what he meant. He drove us to Kazanskh Station to collect our belongings. He decided to wait in the car for us and said "Okay, you're free to go."

I joked and replied, "Yes, free to go to prison." We all laughed.

From here he drove to the Damodedovo, one of the airports in Moscow used by Soviet citizens for internal travel. Moscow has a different airport for government officials and the military, and another terminal for international travel. The KGB man took all our documents with him to try to get our tickets while we waited for him, but after a long time, he returned to explain that he was having difficulties because the flights were very full. "If you wanted a single ticket, there would be no problem." He suggested that we fly to Krasnoyarsk and change planes there. This was a very long journey, and I said that we would rather stay overnight in Moscow and travel later, when things weren't so busy.

Hearing this, the KGB man became quite agitated. "It doesn't matter to me, but you'll lose one day. It's very important that you return immediately to prepare your documents to leave the Soviet Union. It was the first time he had indicated that he knew something more about us. I was surprised by what he said and wondered whether it could be true.

Eventually we compromised and flew to Krasnoyarsk where he arranged with another of his "friends" to assist us. "How will we know him?" I asked the KGB man just before we left him at the airport.

"Don't worry," he replied. "You don't have to know him. He will recognize you. Let all the passengers leave the plane first. Be sure that you are the last to leave the plane."

True to his word, a KGB man in Krasnoyarsk, wearing a grey jacket, was waiting on the runway for us. He quickly ushered us through all the formal procedures and collected our luggage. At Krasnoyarsk we had to transfer to another airport, but over one hundred people were standing in line for the transfer bus parked some distance from the line with the driver smoking. The KGB man talked to the lady selling bus tickets. He then took the driver aside for a private conversation. After a few minutes, the driver climbed aboard the bus. At a given sign the bus driver stopped, and all of us boarded the bus. "Choose any seat you wish," he said to us, gesturing toward an empty vehicle.

The conductress looked a little confused. "Who's going to pay for the lot of you?" I handed over one and a half rubles each for our fare, but the KGB man didn't pay anything.

As the bus approached the regular stop where the people had been waiting, those in the front of the line jostled their way inside. All of them were complaining to the driver about us. They were angry that we were seated inside without having to wait. The driver replied, "Ask the man for the KGB." His words silenced the complaints.

Again the KGB man's persuasive ways were successful. The forty-five minute flight from Krasnoyarsk to Abakan was full, but he managed to find three extra seats for us. The bus journey from Abakan to Chernogorsk was long and uneventful. Galina, Tatyana, and I had been traveling for twenty-four hours. We were tired and hungry. When we reached home, the news was confirmed: our family had been told to prepare our documents for emigration.

Previously we had not been allowed to register our applications; sometimes the officials wouldn't even hand over the forms. Was this another trick?

20

Countdown

Wednesday July 13

Sugochokov, the head of the local KGB in Chernogorsk was smiling. "You have a lot of work to do to prepare your documents for emigration, but don't worry I'll help you."

Was I dreaming? Again the KGB wanted to help us. Why? I couldn't understand what was happening. Two days ago we were on holiday in Moscow. Now everything seemed to have changed.

"We'll arrange special tickets for your travel because it's quite busy now, but leave it to me, we'll get enough tickets for all of you."

I replied that we were tired and that there were too many things for us to complete in time.

"No, it's been decided with Moscow that you'll leave Saturday," he spoke authoritatively. Pausing for a moment, he continued, "If you don't leave Saturday as arranged, I wouldn't like to say what would happen to you." The words were spoken calmly, with no hint of menace or alarm. Instead, he seemed to be cautioning us.

He took us in his car to the police station where we stayed until seven that evening, filling in forms. All of the local governmental departments and administrative offices are linked to the police, so it was quite natural for the KGB chief to take charge of our situation. Yet for us it was a surprise. Why would they want to help people like us? But we were weary from traveling, so we just agreed with them and proceeded to fill in all the forms we were handed.

Thursday July 14

The resident photography studio had made a mistake with our passport photographs. When the KGB man saw that they did not conform with the regulation's requirements, he was furious and forced the photographer to return the money that we had left as a deposit. He demanded to know their names and said, "Who do you work for? I'll be back to deal with you."

Tatyana knew a lady in a photography studio. The three of us raced there in a police car, and she agreed to provide the necessary photographs as a rush job. When the KGB man showed the lady his documents, she was surprised. She said, "Why I've never known such a high official come visit me." She turned to Tatyana and said, "Why didn't you tell me that you had such influential friends. You don't need my help when you know such people."

The photographs were to have been ready by three or three-thirty. The KGB man was pacing up and down the front of the studio. He was very nervous in case the photographs weren't ready on time. But we were in no rush. We were tired from the traveling. The procedure for emigration was complex and required filling in forms and more forms. All of this activity left us even more tired. Why should we rush? We had waited twenty-two years to leave the Soviet Union, we could wait a few more days. But the KGB man seemed to have a deadline, which we knew nothing about.

He seemed happy we were leaving. I was puzzled. We had spent two days with him preparing our documents. In all that time, we only saw him smile and joke. It seemed as though he were our best friend. If we'd been arrested, things would have been very different.

We collected the photos on schedule and then returned to the office before returning to Tatyana's home for a very important date—our marriage! Although our state wedding had been completed on June 17, we wanted a Christian marriage to seal our vows before God. The night before our friends had been informed, and about one hundred people, including my family, gathered in Tatyana's home. It was a simple service followed by a meal together. We had little time to prepare things, but friends helped us. After the short service—barely one and a half hours—our friends congratulated us. Mr. and Mrs. Chmykhalov sounded so strange. Everything had happened so quickly.

Friday July 15

I'm married! It was the only thing I could think of. Somehow I thought I would feel differently, but exactly how, I didn't know. I gazed across the room at Tatyana, while she prepared tea and snacks for us.

"Come here, Mrs. Chmykhalov," I teased her. It took her a moment to realize that I was calling her. We sat together cuddling and giggling. For a moment it seemed like we didn't have a care in the world. I wished that we could spend the day together, but there was still much to be done. There was to be no honeymoon for the newlyweds!

Again we took the same route to the police office where some last minute complications had arisen and more papers had to be located—this time from the factory where Tatyana worked. But at last all the papers and documents and forms were stuffed into a brown paper file, and Tatyana and I set off for Abakan where the documentation had to be submitted to the OVIR (emigration and visa office). We were required to pay seven hundred rubles for each adult person in the form of a customs tax imposed by the government. In addition, one ruble is charged for the passport. We required a passport, only to return it to the Soviet government. The banks handle a special account for this procedure but are closed from twelve to one, so again we had to rush to be there before closing time.

Our family was not rich, and seven thousand rubles was a lot of money. This represented our life's savings after virtually everything we owned had been sold. I handed the money over the counter at the bank and collected the receipt, which we took straight back to the OVIR office. They recognized us immediately and ushered us into a private office.

We had reached the final stages of this strange journey. Wearily I sank into a chair. My feet were aching, and my mouth was dry. We had slept just a few hours each night, and all the days had been busy. Even today we had time to eat only the few snacks that Tatyana had prepared. What would the officials in the OVIR say? I handed over the receipt for seven thousand rubles. Almost immediately they produced our exit visas.

When they handed us our stamped visas, I stared speechlessly at them. The visas were in the names of the head of each family: Peter, Vladimir, and myself. I froze; I just couldn't move. Gently, Tatyana touched my arm. She knew it wasn't over.

From the OVIR we went to the airport to book tickets to Moscow, and then I telephoned the American Embassy in Moscow. "We've received our visas. We're flying into Moscow on Saturday." I could barely whisper the words into the telephone receiver. We returned home around seven in the evening to find that a farewell service had been organized for us. It was time to thank God.

Saturday July 16

The last three days had been spent preparing documents. Now we had our exit visas, and in a few hours we would be in Moscow. I had not stopped to think exactly what all this meant. I suddenly realized that this was to be my last day in Chernogorsk. I was leaving home for the last time. I glanced around the room as a wave of nostalgia hit me. But Tatyana stopped me from day dreaming. "Come on, Tim, we have to pack."

I stood with my hands on my hips. I just couldn't decide what I should take and what had to be left behind. I found myself stopping every little while. Almost every item had some special meaning. We did not have many things, but I felt attached to our few possessions. With a cool sense of reality, Tatyana took charge and quickly filled our two suitcases with an assortment of clothes and personal things. We did not have much money and knew our goods would have to last us a long time.

The news had spread that we were leaving, and as friends dropped in to say good-by, they were offered a choice of objects that were to have been left behind. I closed the door for the last time and didn't look back. There was no time to waste. Tatyana and I hurried to reach the prearranged spot where the bus was to pick us up, but when we reached there, we found it had already left for the airport. Just then, a friend of ours, realizing what had happened, agreed to take us in his car.

I saw Anatoly and Svetlana standing near the customs barrier holding hands. Svetlana had tears in her eyes as my brother spoke softly to her. Both of them had intended to marry, but the orders from Moscow had surprised us all. We had five days to leave Chernogorsk. There was just not enough time for Anatoly and Svetlana to marry because the state requires one month's registration, and they will not accept church weddings as legal.

"Time is impossible to stop and it passes quickly," Anatoly whispered. "I don't know when I will see you again, but I will write to you. I will never forget you."

Another sad farewell was awaiting. Tatyana's mother and sisters, Galina and Nadezhda stood to one side. "Mama," Tatyana said, "when will I see you again?" She clung to her mother in a tearful embrace. Galina and Nadezhda comforted their mother as I came to Tatyana's side and put my arm around her.

Many people had gathered together at the airport terminal to say good-by. All around I could see KGB men watching and taking photographs. Our friends from church were singing special songs and hymns. It was a very emotional time. Some of the people at the airport were puzzled to see the crowd around us and were curious about the singing. They came over to find out what was happening. As they stopped to talk to people from our church, the KGB men stepped in and forced them to move along.

We went through customs at four-thirty to check our hand luggage. As the customs officer who was checking my case finished, he remarked about how many KGB men had come to watch us leave.

We stood in line waiting to enter the plane. Suddenly there was a flurry of activity as militia men rushed past us.

I asked one of the airline staff what was happening and why we were delayed. He replied, "We found a man hiding in the toilet on the plane. We suspect he's a terrorist and that he's planted a bomb on the plane."

I didn't know what to think, but we all tried to stay calm. We were told that our flight to Moscow was now going to be delayed by several hours. First, all the luggage would have to be checked for the bomb. Then we would have to wait for another plane to become available. When we returned to the airport lounge, our friends were still waiting there. When they saw us heading back, they began to cheer aloud. One of the young men called out, "Have you changed your mind? Are you coming back?"

The plane on which we flew developed problems with its tires, which had to be changed at one of the stopovers causing us another two-hour delay.

Sunday July 17

About four o'clock we finally reached Moscow, five hours later than we were scheduled to arrive. One of the Embassy staff had kindly waited for us and helped us transfer to a hotel. Dawn was breaking when we climbed wearily into bed.

"What's going to go wrong next?" I wondered aloud. When I turned to face Tatyana, I saw that she was asleep, but she was smiling. I also smiled, as my mind went over the extraordinary events of the past few days. Outside our hotel room, I could hear a car pull up noisily. Doors were slammed, and the sound of two men talking filtered upward. I closed my eyes and tried to sleep. It was Sunday. Our luggage was required by Soviet customs the day before departure. Still, we reasoned, there would be time to rest in the days ahead.

Monday July 18

Monday. The time had finally come. Today we would leave the Soviet Union. Our last day. I simply couldn't comprehend it.

For the past five days, I had barely slept. Virtually every hour had been spent in preparation for this moment. Everything had happened so quickly, I didn't have time to think about what it meant or what would happen when it was over. There were still last minute things to do.

With Vladimir and Wayne Leininger we had a few calls to make: First, to book tickets to Vienna for our family, and then to collect visas from the Dutch and Austrian Embassies. We had been granted visas for Israel, but the Jewish State has no diplomatic status with the USSR so the Dutch Embassy handles all their negotiations.

In between visits with the two embassies, our car passed the American Embassy on Chaikovskovo Street. One entrance had been sealed, the iron gates closed with padlocks. Outside the other gate, Soviet militia men still patrolled, and inside the archway, a U.S. marine stood on duty inside a postbox. Everyone seemed better prepared for uninvited visitors. I glanced at the basement window. It was in darkness.

Tickets for Vienna were to have been purchased from funds raised by supporters in the West that had been left at the embassy. But this money did not cover the fares for all of us, so Wayne Leininger had to collect more funds from the embassy. This delayed our return to the hotel, where our family was waiting.

As prearranged, our family paid the hotel bill with the last of our savings and traveled directly to the international airport. Several KGB men were waiting in the airport lounge, silently watching the proceedings. Looking around, Tatyana noticed a familiar face. It was the man who had approached us in the park and helped with our transportation back to Chernogorsk.

He walked over to Tatyana and smiled. "Do you have a problem with tickets? Maybe I can help you once again?" he asked. Tatyana smiled.

My father was surprised. He told her, "I didn't know that you knew any KGB men here in Moscow."

Tatyana sat near the window of the airplane, and I sat beside her holding her hand. The Austrian airlines plane was clean and shiny. Everything seemed new. The hostesses were smiling and seemed very friendly. Each wore a little badge that read: "Friendly . . . Austrian."

We were served excellent food. From across the aisle my brother Alexander called out, "I've never seen such nice food on any of the Soviet airlines that we've flown."

The plane was quite empty. Fifteen members in our family were probably the largest single party. When they announced our departure from Moscow and requested us to fasten our seat belts, I said a silent prayer of thanks to God. I felt overjoyed for my parents and for my family. Their two-decade struggle had been won. Most of all I was glad for my brother's children. They would grow up in a country free from persecution. We all knew there would be pressures and problems of a different kind, but our children would grow up in Christian homes where our Lord Jesus would be worshiped in freedom.

When the plane taxied down the runway and lifted itself gracefully into the sky, someone gave a shout of joy. We were in the air.

Praise God!

I looked out the window of the plane. We were flying low over the city of Moscow. All I could see from my seat on the airplane were the tops of buildings. Somewhere, in one of those buildings, I had lived in one basement room for nearly five years. I had been lost in Moscow, and my life had changed. I felt an ache deep in my heart. I was leaving forever the country of my childhood and teenage years, the land of my birth.

AMERICA

1

"It's Like a Dream"

I was too tired to think as I stepped from the plane in Vienna. Twilight cast the airport runway with a warm glow. Below the stairs on the airport's tarmac stood many friends, smiling and waving, some of whom I recognized from their visits to the basement. Reporters, photographers, and television cameras recorded the event. I stood at the top of the stairs for an extra minute, clutching Tatyana's hand tightly. Silently, I thanked God for this moment, this miracle of release. I couldn't believe it was happening.

I can't remember walking down the stairs, but suddenly we were hugging and embracing old friends and new ones. It was an extraordinary moment. One journalist asked me how I felt. I couldn't explain. In English, I couldn't think of the words quickly enough, and in Russian, I didn't think there was a word or phrase that could explain just how I felt or what this meant to our family. I replied, "It's like a dream."

The following day, Tuesday, July 19, my parents, my aunt, my brothers and sisters, and all the children left Vienna for the United States. At the airport in St. Louis, Missouri, about three hundred people, mainly from the United Pentecostal church, had gathered together to welcome them to America. As my parents arrived, the group began to sing, "Hallelujah! He's a prayer-answering God."

Vladimir and Katharina and their four children traveled on to California where they planned to settle down.

Tatyana and I stayed on in Vienna for a few days. Vienna itself is strangely reminiscent of Eastern Europe because it occupies a privileged site bordering East and West. The city's history is matched by its architecture. Down winding streets we passed quaint old churches and huge marble sculptures in town squares. Wandering by the Danube and listening to the gentle strains of familiar waltzes in Strauss Park left us in a kind of daze. Could this really be happening? After waiting so long, everything had happened so fast.

I couldn't forget the past, and memories of our "lost five years" in Moscow came flooding back. Sometimes it is hard to pick out the individual days. Everything seems blurred; the memories are hazy, the images cloudy and distant. Other days I can remember as though they were yesterday. Sometimes a word or phrase triggers my memory, and I find myself traveling to another time.

We waved good-by to Vienna on Friday, after spending five days in the city. Then we flew on to St. Louis where we were reunited with our family, and after a short stay there, we continued our journey on to Dallas for another sojourn. I had accepted a two-year scholarship at Christ For the Nations Institute. A month later, my parents also decided to move to Dallas.

Among Russian Christians there's a saying that suggests that life is like a book with blank pages. Everything we do is marked in the book, both good and bad. With the coming of a new year, we can put the past behind us and turn a new page. We can begin anew, with God's help. For us, beginning a new life in the West was complex. There were many new experiences and new situations, many things were different. Still, we had had a taste of the West during our stay in the embassy. This had served as a transition.

Since our family plans to live and work in America, learning English is a priority for my brothers and sisters. Tatyana and I are awakened by the alarm at six o'clock. Together with fifteen hundred students from all parts of the world who attend the institute, we begin the day with devotions. Mornings are spent attending lectures and studying, while Tatyana helps with young children in the nursery. After classes I work in the circulation department, assisting in the distribution of the monthly magazine, which is sent to thousands.

We have discovered interesting differences between life here and in the USSR. In Chernogorsk, we had walked to the shops to buy food; here we rely on friends to drive us to the shops. At first the huge shops and the tremendous variety and abundance of goods amazed me. Some shops are open all night; the price is always "right" since nearly everything is available on credit. In the USSR, people wrap up most things in newspapers and pages from magazines. In this way, *Pravda* and *Izvestiya* serve a useful purpose. While visiting in England, I purchased a pair of gloves for ninety-nine pence, and the shop gave me a brightly colored plastic bag. This also puzzled me.

On the weekends, Tatyana and I are often invited to share our testimony in churches. As we travel and see America, I am sometimes surprised at what I see.

I had learned about America through reading books and magazines and talking to people during our stay in the embassy. I envisioned America as a nation built by immigrants—people who came from cities and towns and villages all over the world to build a new land where people could live together in freedom, whatever their beliefs or language.

America's grand heritage was its acknowledgment of God. Even its coinage proudly portrayed its beliefs: In God We Trust. I believed that statement. Our family came to America to be a part of that tradition, to take our place in this land.

It is hard for me to understand how easily people forget their traditions and values, even their origins, and the lands from which they came. It's hard when I see those who have arrived as immigrants, as people like us, unwilling to help others who are struggling for the freedom that they now take for granted.

I am surprised to find a tremendous desire for personal affluence and power even in some churches. It seems that as long as everyone can have a good life, we forget about those who may be suffering and in need. There is a Western saying "out of sight, out of mind" translated as being blind and mad. People think that all problems can be solved by personal happiness and personal security, without a thought for others. I feel so hurt when I see people who live for themselves in such a selfish way and forget those who are in need; some even in their own country, in their own town.

We may have impressive churches, many riches, and

great influence. If God grants us these, we should rejoice, but this is no evidence of the presence of God. Scripture exhorts us to be humble in our power, to seek righteousness, to establish justice in our land, and to testify before others that the power of God can change lives. We may be forgotten and ignored by the world, but we will be known by God. A far better recognition will be ours.

This challenge comes to us whether we are in a high office or in a routine desk job, in the home or the factory, in the city or the suburb. In the Soviet Union, we say that we must live by truth. In America, I see different expressions of worship with varied emphases, Christians chasing various dreams with each believing he is right and each one thinking he has God on his side. But Christians must remember there is no monopoly on truth, no new, improved truth. Truth outlives time and man.

2

No Regrets

"What has surprised you the most since you arrived in the West?"

The girl who asked the question was a young college student sitting in the front row of the church where I had been invited to speak. She had a bright, open face and was dressed in blue jeans and a tee shirt. Her blond hair was tied in a pony tail. A badge pinned to her blouse read: "For the best results, follow the maker's instructions." I stopped to think; I had experienced so much since arriving in Vienna. "I was surprised at how many flavors of ice cream you can buy here in America," I joked, and the people in the church began to laugh.

I decided to give her a more serious reply. "I was surprised to find that schools in America and the Soviet Union have one thing in common. In both institutions it is illegal to pray to God. Under the banner of civil liberties and equal rights, Christians have sacrificed those principles basic to the faith. Of course, we must defend the rights of man. But for man, the first right is to worship God."

During our weekend traveling to share testimony, this was typical of many churches in the West: an impressive building, clean and spotless; large comfortable chairs, stained glass windows, extensive recreation and leisure facilities; and people dressed in their best clothes. All around the church flowers had been tastefully arranged; at the front was a simple wooden cross.

As I finished speaking, over a dozen people raised their hands. A scholarly-looking man wearing glasses spoke in a slow southern drawl, "Could we compromise with the Soviets to achieve some success? What is your opinion? If we organize demonstrations and petitions aren't we going to annoy them? Isn't it better to talk quietly and privately with them?"

I had heard this line of argument so many times before. While we were in the embassy, several people had argued that "quiet diplomacy" was the best route to gain any success with the Soviets. So I did not hesitate to reply.

"Only those unfamiliar with the Soviet mentality would seriously consider this as the best tactic. The Soviet government respects strength. There is no other way to deal with them. You may think that you have gained an advantage by compromising. It is not so. They have decided ahead of time just what concessions they will grant. Their posture is tough and uncompromising, a take-it-or-leave-it stance. When the opposition's compromises begin, it is purely one-sided. The Soviet government sees it as weakness. Ultimately, both sides are pleased. One thinks they have achieved a victory by negotiation. The other side gloats at their stupidity."

Almost immediately another young man stood up and spoke, "But should Christians become involved with political issues and human rights?"

I replied, "We can learn from the example of the apostle Paul. Throughout Acts we learn he exercised his rights as a Roman citizen."

I knew this was a question on many people's minds, so I spoke carefully. "To work in a political structure in defense of human rights is the scriptural concept of justice. Our faith demands it of us."

I noticed a girl sitting by the aisle. She had been listening intently to me. Occasionally she scribbled in a paperback notebook. I saw her on the verge of rising to her feet to ask a question, but she remained seated. She was obviously shy and nervous.

"Do you have a question for me?" I asked her. "Don't be shy, this is America, you can speak quite freely here."

People were amused at my little joke, and this put her at ease. Slowly she rose to her feet and spoke in a soft, hesitant voice. "Tim, I have been deeply moved listening to you, but I know in a few days, I will have forgotten a lot of what you have said. I find it difficult to think about a situation so far away. All I can think about are my own problems and my own life. Christians in Siberia seem too far away for me."

I smiled at the girl and tried to understand her dilemma. Her question was at the heart of a central problem confronting the Western church. I had heard similar questions everywhere I had spoken.

I responded, "Each of us is part of the one body of Christ. The body of Christ is separated—in America and Antarctica, in Vietnam and in Ethiopia and Eritrea, in the highlands of Tibet and in New Zealand, in Siberia and in

Santiago. But together we are all members of the body of Christ.

"It's not a question of who has the biggest organization or the most impressive church. It doesn't matter who's the most dynamic speaker or who has the best television ministry with the largest audience ratings. It's not our business to compete with each other. It's our calling to serve each other. If we have been given power, with that goes responsibility. If that is misused or only used for our own glory, then the body of Christ is weakened. Our gifts have been granted to share with the whole body of believers."

I opened my Bible and read aloud from 1 Corinthians 12:12-26.

"If we don't help people in need, who will help us in our need?" I posed the question for the audience. "Our response should not be provoked by duty, guilt, or obligation. It should be a spontaneous act of love and compassion. In helping others, we help ourselves.

"Christians all over the world are suffering for their faith, not just in the Soviet Union. If we caught a glimpse of their pain, we would find it impossible not to help or to become preoccupied with our own little worlds."

I reminded the church of Hebrews 13:3, which encourages us (as the NIV has it) to "remember those in prison as if you were their fellow prisoners and those who are mistreated as if you yourselves were suffering." I said, "Our responsibility is to pray and work. Prayer and action must go together. Just like every human body needs food and water. It's as natural as that." Then I read James 2:14-26.

The meeting had lasted a long time. I was tired, my throat was parched, and I needed a drink. Still, I felt I couldn't stop. I had been granted this privilege of freedom. As long as my strength would last, I felt compelled to appeal for prayer and action for those who were suffering for their faith. I reminded the congregation of the shining example of the Jewish community, how they had rallied together to provide practical support for their suffering brethren.

"It is time for Christians to learn from their example: to forget their differences, to unite together, to mobilize prayer and action on behalf of the church-in-chains. Each time we write to Soviet officials, we must pray that God will change their hearts. If people pray but don't work, God can't arrange these situations."

I looked at the shy girl near the aisle who had asked the question that had prompted this lengthy reply about the body of Christ and our responsibility to those who suffer. "Submit to God and the Holy Spirit will stir your imagination and show you how to help."

Just before the meeting closed for prayer, I read an appeal from thousands of Soviet Pentecostals, requesting help from their brethren in the West:

> We do not believe that the early Christians would feed the animals that devoured their fellow believers in amphitheaters or collaborate with the tormentors of Christ. However, many Christians in the Free World are inadvertently helping the hands of those who are torturing and persecuting God's people in the USSR.

3

Why Were We Released?

Why were we released?

The newspapers and television reports named many reasons. Perhaps the World Council of Churches and the Russian Orthodox churches did intervene. Perhaps there was a top-level secret deal between the US and the USSR. Perhaps Senator Levin's bill in Congress forced the American government to take our case more seriously. Perhaps the pressure and publicity finally reached its target. Perhaps. . . .

I am, however, convinced of one thing. If people had not prayed and worked for us, our case would have never been resolved. We were in an impossible situation. We needed a miracle. As a young couple, Tatyana and I can testify to the power of God. We are living proof that God answers prayer.

Now our hearts are with those Christians who remain in

the USSR. We cannot forget them. Tatyana's mother and two sisters are still in Chernogorsk, waiting for exit visas. Tatyana misses her family. We would like to be together; we would like her family to enjoy the freedom that we now have. I believe that God will change the hearts of officials, that prison gates will open, and that the faithful will be protected. But God needs our prayer and action to play a part.

Only God can work a miracle, but He needs His "miracle workers" here on earth to work out his purposes.

An example and inspiration for our vision has been suggested by St. Ignatius of Loyola, the founder of the Jesuit Fathers: "One must work as if everything depends on you. And one must pray as if everything depends on God."

Time is a funny thing. It can play tricks on you. Time is an enemy to some; a friend to others. Some complain that there are never enough hours in the day; others never know what to do to pass the time.

In Roman times, a day comprised twelve hours measured solely by the length of sunlight, so time varied in length according to place and season. In medieval times, some monks decided to pray at fixed times during the night. This decision led to the invention of a mechanical clock that worked in the dark and altered forever the concept of time in our lives.

I lived four years, nine months, and thirteen days in the basement of the American Embassy in Moscow. Some people are horrified that I spent so much time in the embassy as a teenager. They view the embassy as a thief of time. This is almost more shocking to them than the imprisonment of hundreds of people for their faith and ideas. Some people spend vast amounts of time, energy, and resources on idle pursuits and trivial things; others are merely amused at such extravagance.

Sometimes we come to despise things in our life—relationships in which we feel trapped, situations from which we'd like to escape. We think if only this situation could change, all our problems would be solved, and our life would change. How many times I had dreamed in the embassy that a trap door would be in our basement floor when I awoke. Secretly we could steal out of the corner where we found ourselves. Many of us believe that God can change our lives, so we wait for a miracle. But sometimes the real miracle is when we, not our situation, change.

The years in the embassy were not easy. There were times when I became disillusioned and angry. But during that time, the reality of God's presence became my experience. For five years our situation in the American Embassy in Moscow didn't change. But I did.

If life were a book and I could turn back the pages of history, and should I find myself once again on Chaikovskovo Street, I would change nothing; I have no regrets.

Conclusion: A Time Such as This

Our family first tried to leave the Soviet Union in 1963. I was a babe, just one year old. On July 18, 1983, that dream came true. We received exit visas for fifteen people, our entire family. But actually sixteen people are now in the West. Katharina gave birth to a lovely baby boy, one month after they arrived in America. They named him Emmanuel, which means "God with us." One year later they had another baby boy named Pauel.

When I first arrived in Vienna, I thought I was dreaming. I couldn't believe it was happening. During the next few months there were still times when I would wake in the middle of the night and imagine I was back in Chernogorsk or in the basement expecting to see a Soviet militia man's face at the window. One day something happened that made me fully realize I wasn't dreaming. We had left the Soviet Union and were living in a free country.

I walked into a downtown Dallas bookstore. For a few dollars I purchased a children's Bible. I walked out of the store and down the street clutching the open Bible in my hand. I was smiling. I knew people who passed me were giving me some strange looks. I don't think they understood what joy I felt buying this Bible.

A few days earlier Tatyana had told me very precious news: I was going to be a father. Together we knelt in our apartment and thanked God for this gift. Our eyes were wet; our hearts joyful. The children's Bible was for our unborn child and with it went my prayer that our child would grow up to honor its word and to live by its truth.

When our darling Rebekah was born on August 18, 1984, I felt that for such a moment as this our family had struggled. What had seemed like a dream fro twenty years was now a reality. *Thank God!*

On August 21, 1985, Rachel was born in the Parkland hospital. We praise God that He has sent us these two beautiful girls, who will be able to grow up in a free country and will be able to study freely the Word of God.

Acknowledgments

I know that many people and organizations helped me during our stay in the American Embassy. I am grateful to each one. I am also thankful to those people who prayed for us and petitioned the authorities. God used each one to arrange a miracle of release.

I have listed here those organizations that I have met and heard about since our arrival in the West. I hope, in time, others will make themselves known to me.

Australia: Owen Salter, *On Being* Magazine. *Britain:* Peter Meadows, *Buzz* Magazine; Michael Rowe, Keston College; Bryce Cooks, Piccadilly Radio; Danny Smith, Campaign to Free the Siberian Seven. *Finland:* Pirkko Huuhtanen, Patmos International. *France:* Philip Draun de Guise, Faith and Action. *Germany:* Yuri Belov, International Association for Human Rights. *Holland:* Dirk Jan Groot, Christian Foundation for Conscience Convicts; L. P. Dorenbos, E. O. Television; Andre Ceelen. *Ireland:* David Turner, Christian Concern. *Sweden:* Vilgot Fritzon, Slaviska Missionen; Mrs. Betsy Ramsey; Tore Nilsson, MP *Switzerland:* Marianne Ridge, Christian Solidarity International. USA: Olga and Blahsov Hruby, Religion in Communist Dominated Lands; Jane Drake, SAVE; Mrs. Freda Lindsey, Christ For The Nations; Mike MacIntosh, Horizon Fellowship; Jeff Collins, Steve Lawson, East–West News Service.

In addition, my sincere thanks to: Senator Carl Levin,

Senators Alan Simpson, Joseph R. Biden, and Charles Grassley; Representative and Mrs. Tom Lantos, Representatives Barney Frank and Michael Barnes; Congressmen Don Bonker, Richard Shelby, and Bill Dickinson; British MP's including David Alton, David Atkinson, and George Robertson. Swedish MP's Per-Olof Strindberg, Elisabeth Fleetwood, Stina Eliasson, Rolf Sellgren, Borje Stensson, Stina Anderson, Tore Nilsson, Sven Johansson, Tage Adolfsson. Also Myrna Grant, Paul and Annette Roush, Kent Hill, Lynn Buzzard, Mark Gitenstein, Sister Ann Gillen, Anne Shipps, Harry Jones, Babette Wampold, Colleen and Betty Littell, Rev. William Villaume, Isabella T. Hessell, Janet and Roger Stanley, Linda Fletcher, Arlo and Karen Blumhagen, Eric Hockstein, Leslie Powell, Rev. John Pollock, Oliver Sampson, Dough Kahn, and Rev. John Wildrianne, Earl S. Poysti, Vera Kuschnir. I would also like to thank Vladimir Bukovsky and Alexander Ginzburg for their support.

The Last Christian is not intended to be a final, comprehensive, conclusive, or definitive version of our stay for four years, nine months, and thirteen days in the American Embassy in Moscow. Neither does it purport to represent the view of all seven of us in the embassy. If seven people experience something together, there will inevitably be seven different opinions of that moment. I am not a spokesman for "the Siberian Seven."

The Last Christian is my opinion, my impression of a time that changed my life forever.

Timothy Chmykhalov

I didn't know that a telephone call from Peter Meadows would change my life so dramatically. Acting on the idea from Dan Wooding, Peter launched the Campaign to Free the Siberian Seven and invited my involvement. I agreed with these limitations: three-and-a-half days a week and strictly for two months.

But that was May 1981, and for me, life would never be quite the same again.

There will be another time to thank those many, special people who helped us during our three year campaign. Here I would like to thank those who helped Timothy and me during the preparation of this book. For advice, counsel, assistance, support, dictionaries, and the gift of friendship: Mum and Clement, Paul and Margaret Evans, the Cobham Fellowship, Dirk Jan Groot, Emma and Raj Foa-Sacranie, Stewart and Carol Henderson, John Hunt, Edward England, and of course, Gerald and Anona Coates. And to Joan, whom I first met dressed in a Russian costume at a Siberian Seven "birthday party" on Fleet Street, and who, three years later, brought her love and support to share with me in our own campaign.

Danny Smith

Notes

1. I am grateful for information from many sources, including Henrick Smith, "The Russians," 1976.

2. Yuri Belov served fifteen years in prisons, psychiatric hospitals, and labor camps before he was exiled. At one point he was declared clinically dead. Alexandr Solzhenitsyn noted that Yuri was imprisoned to be "cured of his religious beliefs." He now lives in West Germany and is head of the Soviet department at the International Association for Human Rights.

3. From the newspaper *Kholhozneo Selo,* January 1, 1961.

4. The issue of registration of churches can be examined further by studying information from such sources as Keston College in England and Religion in Communist Dominated Lands in New York.

5. Acts 5:27–29, NIV.

6. John Barron, *The KGB: The Secret Work of Soviet Secret Agents* (Readers Digest Press, 1974).

7. *The Chronicle of the Lithuanian Catholic Church* (published as booklets), 351 Highland Boulevard, Brooklyn, New York 11207, USA. See also Michael Bourdeaux, *Land of Crosses* (1979).

8. Information on life and conditions in Soviet labor camps can be found in several publications including: "Prisoners of Conscience in the USSR: Their treatment and conditions," Amnesty International Newsletter, XIV, no. 2 (February 1984).

9. Alexandr I. Solzhenitsyn, *The Gulag Archipelago. 1918–1956. An Experiment in Literary Investigation.* (New York: Harper & Row, 1974).

10. Ibid, pp. 540-41: "In 1937 there were no latrine buckets in certain Siberian prisons or there weren't enough. Not enough of them had been made ahead of time. Siberian industry hadn't caught up with the scope of arrests. So if long ago the Minusinsk prison had been built for five hundred people . . . and there were now ten thousand in it, it meant that each latrine bucket ought to have become twenty times bigger. But it had not.

"If they only knew about the scheme of things in that same Minusinsk prison: there was only one food bowl for every four prisoners; and only one mug of drinking water per day was issued to each (there weren't enough mugs to go around). And it could happen that one of the four contrived to use the bowl allotted to him and three others to relieve his internal pressure and then refuse to hand over his daily water ration to wash it out for lunch. What a conflict! What a clash of four personalities! What nuances! And I am not joking. That is when the rock bottom of a human being is revealed.

"Russian pens are too busy to write about it, and Russian eyes don't have time to read about it. I am not joking—because only doctors can tell us how months in such a cell will ruin a human being's health for his entire life."

11. Ibid. p. 584: "In Minusinsk in 194-, after the prisoners had not been taken out into the fresh air for a whole year, they had forgotten how to walk, to breathe, to look at the light. And then they took them out, put them in formation, and drove them the fifteen miles to Abakan on foot. About a dozen of them died along the way and no one is ever going to write a great novel about it, not even one chapter: if you live in a graveyard, you can't weep for everyone."

12. Eduard Kuznetsov, *Prison Diaries* (London: Vallentine, Mitchell, 1975), p. 170.

13. Anatoly Marchenko, *My Testimony* (Pall Mall Press, 1969), p. 151.

14. Deuteronomy 33:25 NIV.

15. A book of secret Soviet laws on religion is now on file at Keston College. The book, entitled *Legislation on Religious Cults (Collection of Materials and Documents)* was published by

"Yuridicheskaya Literatura" Moscow in 1971. It was edited by V. A. Kuroedov, the chairman of the Council for Religious Affairs and by A. Only" (Diya Sluzhebnogo Polsovaniya), and to restrict its circulation each of the 21,000 copies were numbered. The number in the Xerox copy now in the West has been erased and therefore cannot be traced.

16. Vladimir Bukovsky, *To Build a Castle* (New York: Viking Penguin Inc., 1978).

17. Ibid.

18. Andrei Amalrik, *Involuntary Exile into Siberia* (New York: Harper & Row and the Alexander Herzen Foundation, 1970).

19. For factual and objective information on Christianity and church life inside the USSR, readers are advised to consult sources such as Keston College in England and Religion in Communist Dominated Lands in the USA.

20. Oleg Bitov, *Sunday Telegraph*, February 12, 1984.

21. *The Chronicle of Current Events* is in the journal of the movement for the defense of human rights in the USSR. In spite of KGB attempts to suppress it, the journal is still regularly produced in typescript samizdat inside the Soviet Union and circulated on the chain letter principle. Copies of the *Chronicle* can be obtained from Amnesty International.

22. Stalin, *Works*, X, (1927), pp. 132-133.

23. Lenin, *Attitude of the Workers Party with Regard to Religion*, (1909).

24. Lenin, *ABC of Communism*, (1906).

25. Lenin, *Attitude of the Workers Party with Regard to Religion*, (1909).

26. Ibid.

27. Lounatcharski (Commissaire for Public Education, 1933), *New Anti-religious Manual*.

28. Lenin, *Socialism and Religion*, (1905).

29. Leonid Brezhnev signed the Helsinki Final Act in Helsinki on August 1, 1975.

30. In *The Siberian Seven,* John Pollock notes that "The Vashchenko Invitation came in the name of Reverend Cecil J. Williamson, Jr., pastor of the Crescent Hill Presbyterian Church, Selma, Alabama. A visiting preacher had emphasized the plight of Russian evangelicals. The church offered to sponsor any one of the many Pentecostal families wishing to emigrate; the Tolstoy Foundation in New York informed Williamson, late in December 1977, that his church had been assigned the Vashchenko family in Chernogorsk, Siberia. The church officers filled in the necessary papers. The Invitation took four months to reach the Vashchenkos. It arrived through the international mail on April 20, 1978.''

31. They left the embassy on October 31, 1978, and it was reported that she joined her mother in the USA in 1979.

32. John Pollock, *The Christians from Siberia* (London: Hodder and Stoughton, 1964). American title: *The Faith of the Russian Evangelicals* (New York: McGraw-Hill, 1964); paperback edition, Zondervan, 1969, reissued 1972 as *Faith and Freedom in Russia).*

33. Between January and March 1981.

34. This event took place about the middle of August. It is described in Frank Church's US Senate Report, October 16, 1980, p. 45.

35. John Pollock, *The Siberian Seven* (Waco, Texas: Word Books, 1980).

36. S.2890 was reintroduced as S.312 in the US Senate by Carl Levin in the new session. Congressional Record, No. 108-part II, volume 126, Washington, June 27, 1980.

37. The entire text of the appeal letter to President Brezhnev is included in the Congressional Record of S.2890.

38. Senator Church's US Senate Report, p. 43.

39. The right of asylum contained in the Universal Declaration of Human Rights 1948 states: 14 (1) ''Everyone has the right to seek and enjoy in other countries asylum from persecution.''

40. Senator Howard Baker's letter is included in Frank Church's US Senate Report, see p. 35.

41. First press conference was held on January 8, 1982 during Lidiya Vashchenko's hunger strike.

42. Ibid.

43. Kevin Lynch, articles in *National Review* (August 31, 1979; March 21, 1980; April 3, 1981).

44. Ibid.

45. *Sunday Express*, London, February 1, 1982.

46. Ibid.

47. *Time* Magazine, (June 4, 1979).

48. *The Peace Movement and the Soviet Union* first appeared as an article in *Commentary Magazine* in May 1982. The booklet, which was published by the Coalition for Peace Through Security (London) is also included in *Who is for Peace?* by Vladimir Bukovsky (Nashville: Thomas Nelson Publishers). See also "Better Red than Dead is not Good Enough," *The Times*, London, December 4, 1981.

49. Jeremiah 6:13 and 8:11, NIV.

50. Interview with BBC Television March 1, 1976. Text published as *Warning to the Western World* (Salem, New Hampshire: The Bodley Head, 1976).

51. Ibid.

52. Vasily Barats is the founder of the Committee for the Right to Emigrate. He was sentenced in March 1983 to five years' imprisonment; His wife Galina was sentenced to six years' imprisonment and three years' exile in June 1983. Both are Pentecostal Christians.

53. Michael Bourdeaux, "Some Personal Reflections," Issue no. 147 Keston News Service (April 22, 1982). Reprinted in *Church of England Newspaper*, London.

54. Lyuba Vashchenko's letter to Dr. Billy Graham was dated April 12, 1982.

55. "Vantage Point," Radio Moscow Broadcast, August 4, 1982. Commentator: Boris Bolitsky; Subject: Religious Freedom.

56. *Time* Magazine (May, 24, 1982). *Newsweek* Magazine (May 24, 1982).
57. Leonid Vladimirov, *Glavit: How the Soviet Censor Works, Index of Censorship,* 1, no. 3/4, (Autumn-Winter 1972), pp. 31–43.
58. Barron, *The KGB.*
59. Ibid.
60. Ibid.
61. The invitations that we received were as follows: 1978, Mrs. Freida Lindsey, Christ for the Nations; 1980, the Blumhagen Family; 1982, Rev. Nathaniel Urshan; 1983, Rev. John Wildrianne, Assemblies of God in Britain.

Appendices and a Final Note

A) Soviet Constitution
B) Universal Declaration of Human Rights
C) Helsinki Final Act
D) Letters from Timothy Chmykhalov
   i) June 27, 1981: Appeal to President Brezhnev
   ii) May 5, 1982: Appeal to Dr. Billy Graham
E) A Final Note

APPENDIX A: SOVIET CONSTITUTION

USSR Constitution of 1977

Article 52
Citizens of the USSR are guaranteed freedom of conscience that is, the right to profess any religion or to profess no religion at all, and to perform religious rites, or to conduct atheist propaganda. The incitement of hostility and hatred in connection with religious beliefs is prohibited.
The church in the USSR is separated from the state, and the school from the church.

Article 54
Citizens of the USSR are guaranteed the inviolability of the person. No one may be arrested unless on the basis of a court order or with the sanction of the procurator.

Article 55
Citizens of the USSR are guaranteed the inviolability of the home. No one has the right, without lawful grounds, to enter a home against the will of the person resident therein.

Article 56
The private life of citizens and the secrecy of correspondence, telephone conversations, and telegraph messages are protected by law.

APPENDIX B: UNIVERSAL DECLARATION OF HUMAN RIGHTS
Approved by the General Assembly of the United Nations, December 10, 1948

Article 13 (1)
Everyone has the right to freedom of movement and residence within the borders of each state.

Article 13 (2)
Everyone has the right to leave any country including his own, and to return to his country.

Article 14 (1)
Everyone has the right to seek and to enjoy in other countries asylum from persecution.

Article 18
Everyone has the right to freedom of thought, conscience, and religion; this right includes freedom to change his religion or belief, and freedom, either alone or in community with others and in public or private, to manifest his religion or belief in teaching, practice, worship and observance.

Article 19
Everyone has the right to freedom of opinion and expression; this right includes freedom to hold opinions without interference and to seek, receive, and impart information and ideas through any media and regardless of frontiers.

Article 20
Everyone has the right to freedom of peaceful assembly and association.

Article 26/3
Parents have a prior right to choose the kind of education that shall be given to their children.

APPENDIX C: HELSINKI FINAL ACT
August 1, 1975

VII

The participating States will respect human rights and fundamental freedoms, including the freedom of thought, conscience, religion or belief, for all without distinction as to race, sex, language, or religion.

Within this framework the participating States will recognize and respect the freedom of the individual to profess and practice, alone or in community with others, religion or belief in accordance with the dictates of his own conscience. In the field of human rights and fundamental freedoms, the participating States will act in conformity with the purposes and principles of the Charter of the United Nations and with the Universal Declarations of Human Rights. They will also fulfill their obligations as set forth in the international declarations and agreements in this field, including inter alia the International Covenants on Human Rights by which they may be bound.

X. Paragraph 5

The participating States make it their aim to facilitate freer movement and contacts, individually and collectively, whether privately or officially, among persons, institutions and organizations of the participating States, and to contribute to the solution of the humanitarian problems that arise in that connection. d) Travel for Personal or Professional Reasons: The participating States intend to facilitate wider travel by their citizens for personal or professional reasons.

Paragraph 7

They confirm that religious faiths, institutions, and organizations practicing within the constitutional framework of the participating States and their representatives can, in the field of their activities, have contacts and meetings among themselves and exchange information.

APPENDIX D: LETTERS FROM TIMOTHY CHMYKHALOV

Moscow Embassy of the USA
June 27, 1981

President
The Presidium Supreme Soviet, USSR
L. I. Brezhnev
Request

I want to write you a letter and repeat our request to you, that you allow our family to emigrate from the USSR. We asked permission to emigrate 18 years ago. In these years my parents suffered repressions because they wanted to refuse Soviet citizenship (i.e. from the Soviet passports) and also wanted to emigrate from the USSR. These actions brought them repressions from the Soviet authorities.

The first time my father was exiled for one year; the second time he served in a labor camp for one year.

My aunt, Anna Makarenko, was sentenced three times. (Each time for one year, and each time she served in a labor camp.) All this happened because they refused Soviet passports and asked to emigrate from the USSR.

Despite all that, our family continues to ask you to take from us Soviet citizenship and that you permit us to emigrate from the USSR to the USA or Israel.

The authorities continued to persecute us, and my parents sometimes tried to make compromises. I don't want to deceive anyone, and I don't want to do what is against my conscience. Therefore, I have decided not to go into the Army, and I don't want to be a Soviet citizen.

Citizenship should be taken away by the government, but a man should be able to express his will, to have it or not, although it should not be taken away from him. Because of that, the man subjects himself to repressions. For those Believers who decide to follow Christ, the atheistic world promises nothing good.

Our family continues to ask the Soviet government to allow us to emigrate on the religious basis. We ask you to please consider our request.
Chmykhalov Family.

Moscow USSR
Embassy of the USA
May 5, 1982

Dear Dr. Billy Graham,

Request

We turn to you with our appeal to help us emigrate from the Soviet Union to Israel or the USA or to another non-Communist country.

Our family has been asking for permission to emigrate from the USSR for 19 years, on the grounds of our religious convictions, but have not received it up to this time. For this our family has been repressed: my father spent two one-year terms and my aunt spent three one-year terms in the camps. Still we have not achieved emigration from the USSR.

We came to the American Embassy on June 27, 1978, because they had gathered evidence to put my family on trial since we renounce Soviet citizenship and ask permission to emigrate. Now we have been in the embassy almost 4 years, but have not received emigration.

We refuse to be citizens of this country because the government of this country represses us for wanting to fulfill the teachings of Christ.

I refuse to enter the army because it would be against my conscience and religious convictions. Because God says, "Thou shalt not kill" and "Do not take a false oath" (Matt. 5:21, 34).

On March 11, 1982 two men came to our home in Chernogorsk, one by the name of Borisenko. (He works at the Voenkomat, a sergeant-major by rank.) They came in order to issue me a subpoena to appear at the Voenkomat in order to induct me into the army. But because I am here, they didn't give up the subpoena.

This emphasizes that the local authorities had prepared all the documents so that they could imprison us upon our return to Chernogorsk even for the purpose of drawing up an invitation to emigrate from the USSR.

You intend to come to Moscow for the Peace Conference and the question of our emigration is not resolved, but how can one talk of peace and freedom when our problem shows that freedom does not exist in the Soviet Union.

We ask you to request the Soviet government (authorities) to allow us to emigrate from the USSR while the conference is going on. With that they could exhibit freedom in reality. But if the Soviets tell you we must return to Chernogorsk and prepare the visa documents from there, we then want to ask you to tell them that they should issue exit visas for our family who is now in Chernogorsk. Then when we learn that part of the family is in America, since they have invitations from the USA, or in another country, we will leave the embassy to draw up the documentation for emigration to be reunited with our family.

Please don't refuse our request. Help us leave the USSR.

Chmykhalov Family.

A FINAL NOTE

Timothy Chmykhalov welcomes correspondence from people who were actively involved in the campaign for his release and those who wish to keep in touch with his new life in the West. Timothy, Tatyana, Rebekah, and Rachel—the newest addition to their family—are currently living in Dallas, Texas. It is Timothy's intention to present further information to enable Christians in the West to understand the life of believers inside the Soviet Union today. And at the time of this book's publication in the United States, there is one part of Timothy and Tatyana's family story that remains incomplete. Alexandra, Tatyana's widowed mother, and Galina and Nadezhda, her two sisters, still reside in the Soviet Union. In September of 1984 the Chmykhalovs sent them the proper invitations to come to the United States to live and worship in freedom. The Soviet government refused to issue exit visas.

Timothy Chmykhalov
PO Box 224605
Dallas, Texas 75222
USA

Copies of Senator Carl Levin's US Senate Bill S.312 can be ordered directly from Timothy or the address below. Details of the continuing activities of the Siberian Seven Committee are also available. For further information on how to help Tatyana's family and other Christians suffering for their faith, write to the address below:

Siberian Seven Committee
c/o Pioneer Enterprise
Box 80
Cobham
Surrey KT11 2BQ
Great Britain